My Happiness Habit Journal

ANGELICA RIBEIRO

ISBN-10: 1719251096
ISBN-13: 978-1719251099

Contents

My Happiness Habit Journal belongs to

_____

One

WHY YOU SHOULD USE MY HAPPINESS HABIT JOURNAL

The difference among people's happiness can be explained by their genetic makeup (50 percent), life circumstances (10 percent), and behavior (40 percent).[1] It indicates that we may not be 100 percent in control of our happiness, but we can still control a great portion of it. In other words, it is up to us to spend that 40 percent in choices that will lead us to feeling good.

We don't need to wait for a big package, such as the purchase of a car, to be happier. Although those big packages contribute to our happiness, we can have small packages full of happiness delivered to us every single day. Small happiness packages are delivered to us through the practice of habits based on our principles and beliefs that match our own life expectations. Again, it's up to us to make the choice of practicing such habits.

With that said, to live a more purposeful and mindful life, I encourage you to create lasting positive changes through habits or rituals. As Tal Ben-Shahar, author of books in the field of positive psychology, said, "If we want to enjoy lasting-change, we have to introduce rituals; otherwise the change is temporary and very often

---

[1] Sonja Lyubomirsky, *The How of Happiness: A New Approach to Getting the Life You Want* (New York: Penguin Books, 2007).

disappears."[2]

To help you create lasting positive changes through habits, I invite you to use the components of *My Happiness Habit Journal*. Based on my own experience and on the works of experts and authors on happiness, My Happiness Habit Journal has the potential to lead you to

- develop more self-knowledge;
- identify what makes you happier;
- take responsibility for your happiness;
- better control your stress;
- feel more courageous, especially when facing challenging situations;
- live a more purposeful and mindful life; and
- create long-lasting happiness.[3]

---

[2] Tal Ben-Shahar, "Optimize Interview: Positive Psychology 101," interview by Brian Johnson, Optimize, June 9, 2015, video, 44:45,
https://www.youtube.com/watch?v=jTT7mJCpVq0.

[3] Angelica Ribeiro, *Running into Happiness: How My Happiness Habit Journal Created Lasting Happiness in the Midst of a Crazy-busy Semester* (North Charleston: CreateSpace Independent Publishing Platform, 2018).

Two

COMPONENTS OF MY HAPPINESS HABIT JOURNAL

Here I present each component of My Happiness Habit Journal by stating its purpose, explaining what to do to apply it, providing examples to illustrate how it is used, and informing where it can be found in the journal.

Part I: To be filled out in the morning

1. Happiness-source goals[4]

There are four happiness-source goals: meaningful, pleasurable, challenging, and unpleasurable.

---

[4] Tal Ben-Shahar, *Happier: Learn the Secrets to Daily Joy and Lasting Fulfillment* (New York: McGraw-Hill, 2007).

Pleasurable and meaningful happiness-source goals:

Purpose:
Encourage you to think of two good actions you plan to experience that day. Knowing that your brain does not distinguish reality from imagination, your thoughts anticipate similar good feelings that you will feel when you actually perform those actions.

What to do:
Identify one meaningful and one pleasurable action you plan to do that day. Since some actions can be meaningful and pleasurable, it is OK if these two happiness-source goals overlap.

Examples:
- Pleasurable goal: Watch the new season of *Gilmore Girls*.
- Meaningful goal: Answer my niece's text messages.
- Meaningful and pleasurable goal: Have lunch and talk with my friends Vanessa and Wei.

Unpleasurable and challenging happiness-source goals:

Purpose:
Encourage you to shift your perspective on particular actions from negative to positive. In other words, when doing these tasks, you should not focus on the fact that you dislike them or that they are difficult tasks to be completed. Instead, you should focus on the idea that they are sources of happiness, since they will bring you good feelings in the end.

What to do:
Identify one unpleasurable and one challenging action you have to do that day. They should be actions that will bring you good feelings once they are completed. Since some actions can be challenging and unpleasurable, it is OK if your happiness-source goals for these two categories overlap.

Examples:
- Challenging goal: Prepare and deliver a speech.
- Unpleasurable goal: Clean the house.
- Challenging and unpleasurable goal: Study for the statistics exam.

Where to find this component:
You can find *Happiness-source goals* in the Daily Journal section.

2. Gratitudes[5]

Purpose:
Create a positive mind by training your mind to search for good things. As a result of training your mind to scan for the good, you become a more optimistic person. For example, when faced with problems, your mind automatically looks for positive things, helping you make better decisions and see positive realities (than if your brain was functioning at a neutral or negative state).

What to do:
Think about the last twenty-four hours and write down three things for which you are grateful. The gratitudes can be small or big. Avoid repeating the same gratitudes from day to day in order to force your mind to search for more good things in your life.

Examples:
- I'm grateful for the delicious salad I had for lunch.
- I'm grateful for the time I spent with my nephews.

Where to find this component:
You can find *Gratitudes* in the Daily Journal section.

---

[5] Shawn Achor, *The Happiness Advantage: The Seven Principles that Fuel Success and Performance at Work* (New York: Virgin: Books, 2011).

Part II: To be filled out at night

3. Circle of life[6]

The circle of life involves the following areas: *health, social, relationship with a significant other, family, spiritual, emotional, professional, financial, intellectual,* and *service*.

Purpose:
Encourage you to develop more self-knowledge in terms of how you can regularly address each area of the circle to bring you a more balanced and happier life.

What to do:
Create one or more small concrete goals for each area of the circle of life. You don't have to change your goals often, but you can if you wish. At the end of the day, check the areas of the circle of life that you addressed that day. You should only check the areas from which you performed at least one of the goals. For example, let's say that *exercise* and *eat a healthy snack* were two goals you set for the *health* area of life. On a particular day, you exercised but didn't eat a healthy snack. Although you didn't perform both goals, you still check the *health* area because you performed at least one of its goals.

Examples:
- *Health*—Eat a piece of fruit for a snack.
- *Social*—Send a text message to a friend.
- *Relationship with a significant other*—Compliment him or her.
- *Family*—Start a conversation with my family during dinner.
- *Spiritual*—Say a prayer before going to bed.
- *Emotional*—Meditate; fill out My Happiness Habit Journal.

---

[6] Paulo Vieira, "Coaching: Prosperidade de vida" (Coaching: Prosperity of Life), published September 2013, video, 22:48, https://www.youtube.com/watch?v=nGu7obxmxI0.

- *Professional*—Create lesson plans; grade assignments.
- *Financial*—Keep track of my expenses; deposit ten dollars in my savings account.
- *Intellectual*—Read a book; watch the news.
- *Service*—Compliment, help, or thank someone.

Where to find this component:
You can find *Circle of life* in the Circle of Life section.

4. Happy moments[7]

Purpose:
Encourage you to scan for your positive experiences, notice good things that happened to you, and identify your happiness boosters. Moreover, writing down two happy moments you had makes you relive those moments, bringing the same good feelings you felt when you experienced them.

What to do:
Write down two sentences to describe two happy moments you had during the day (one sentence for each happy moment).

Examples:
- Today I felt happy when I had a meaningful conversation with my friends Val and Shanna.
- Running into Theresa and Yvonne at the conference made me very happy today.

Where to find this component:
You can find *Happy moments* in the Daily Journal section.

---

[7] Tal Ben-Shahar, *Happier: Learn the Secrets to Daily Joy and Lasting Fulfillment* (New York: McGraw-Hill, 2007).

5. A conscious struggle

Purpose:
Help you realize what you need to improve so that you can try to implement it on the following days.

What to do:
Write something you noticed that you want to improve in order to feel better about yourself.

Examples:
- Be more patient with others.
- Smile more.

Where to find this component:
You can find *A conscious struggle* in the Daily Journal section.

6. My commandments[8]

Purpose:
Encourage you to reflect on values and principles you want to practice in life and remind you to keep acting according to them.

What to do:
Create commandments, that is, principles you want for your life. You can create as many commandments as you wish.

Examples:
- Be confident.
- Be grateful.

Where to find this component:
You can find *My commandments* in the My Commandments section.

---

[8] Gretchen Rubin, *The Happiness Project: Or, Why I Spent a Year Trying to Sing in the Morning, Clean My Closets, Fight Right, Read Aristotle, and Generally Have More Fun* (New York: HarperCollins Publishers, 2009).

7. Resolutions[9]

Purpose:
Encourage you to practice new habits that will boost your happiness.

What to do:
In the beginning of each month, based on what can make you happier, create resolutions or new habits (no more than three) you would like to incorporate into your daily routine. At the end of the day, check the resolutions that you accomplished during the day. Once a new month begins, create new resolutions and carry out the ones from previous months.

Examples:
- Read for twenty minutes.
- Play the piano.

Where to find this component:
You can find *Resolutions* in the Resolutions section.

8. Tiny habits[10]

Purpose:
Encourage you to practice new habits that will boost your happiness. This activity is very similar to the resolution one. The difference between tiny habits and resolutions is that the tiny habit involves a small habit (as the name suggests), and it is triggered by a habit you already have.

---

[9] Ibid.
[10] B. J. Fogg, "Forget Big Change, Start With a Tiny Habit," published December 2012 TEDxFremont, Fremont, CA, video, 17:23, https://www.youtube.com/watch?v=AdKUJxjn-R8.

What to do:
In the beginning of each month, create new tiny habits (no more than three) that you would like to incorporate into your daily routine. Create the tiny habits by attaching them to habits you already have. Use the following sentence structure to create a new tiny habit: *After I...* (a habit you already have), *I will...* (the new tiny habit). At the end of the day, check the tiny habits that you accomplished during the day. Once a new month begins, if you want, create new tiny habits and carry out the previous month's tiny habits.

Examples:
- After I eat breakfast, I will write three things I am grateful for.
- After I exercise, I will meditate for five minutes.

Where to find this component:
You can find *Tiny habits* in the Tiny Habits section.

9. An accomplishment

Purpose:
Bring you good feelings due to chemicals (e.g., dopamine) that accomplishments release into your body.

What to do:
Identify an accomplishment you had on that day. The accomplishment can be small or big, significant or insignificant.

Examples:
- I sent out all the thank-you cards.
- I submitted a manuscript to a journal.

Where to find this component:
You can find *An accomplishment* in the Daily Journal section.

10. An act of kindness[11]

Purpose:
Make someone feel good and smile, and contribute to making the world a better place.

What to do:
Perform an act of kindness every day. The act of kindness can be to help, thank, or offer a genuine compliment to someone.

Examples:
- I helped Leily plan her week, and that made her feel less overwhelmed.
- I texted Melika to say that I really appreciated her feedback on my writing.

Where to find this component:
You can find *An act of kindness* in the Daily Journal section.

11. Spiritual master[12]

Purpose:
Imitate your spiritual master in order to strengthen your attitudes and ways of thinking, especially when facing challenging situations.

What to do:
Select someone to be your spiritual master, that is, someone whose traits and attitudes you admire and would like to acquire. Your spiritual master can be anyone—famous or not, alive or not. It can be a saint, an actor or actress, a teacher, a writer, a family member, or a friend. Always keep your spiritual master in mind to serve you as an inspiration on how to act, think, and grow as a person.

---

[11] Shawn Achor, *The Happiness Advantage: The Seven Principles that Fuel Success and Performance at Work* (New York: Virgin: Books, 2011).

[12] Gretchen Rubin, *The Happiness Project: Or, Why I Spent a Year Trying to Sing in the Morning, Clean My Closets, Fight Right, Read Aristotle, and Generally Have More Fun* (New York: HarperCollins Publishers, 2009).

Example:

- My spiritual master is my grandmother.

Where to find this component:
You can find *Spiritual master* in the Spiritual Master section.

12. Overall day rating

Purpose:
Reflect on how you felt throughout the day. By doing so, you will get to know yourself better as to what actions and thoughts can lead you to positive, neutral, and negative feelings.

What to do:
Think about your day; then, rate it by circling the happy, neutral, or sad face.

Example:

Where to find this component:
You can find *Overall day rating* in the Daily Journal section.

13. Happiness Trophy

Purpose:
Relive the good moments you had during the week as you scan for the happiest one. Your mind doesn't distinguish reality from imagination. So when you relive happy moments, you again feel the good feelings you felt when you first experienced them.

What to do:
On Sunday, think about the good moments you had during the week. Identify the happiest moment; the Happiness Trophy goes to the person with whom you spent that moment. Let that person know that you spent the happiest moment of your week with him or her.

Examples:
- "My happiest moment this week was when I got a new toy. So my Happiness Trophy goes to my father because I was with him. He was the one who took me to the store and gave me the toy." Vitor, my eleven-year-old nephew, shared this with me when I asked to whom he would give his Happiness Trophy.
- One day I told my friend Diana, "My Happiness Trophy goes to you. Having a meaningful conversation with you was my happiest moment this week."

Where to find this component:
You can find *Happiness Trophy* in the Daily Journal section.

The purpose of My Happiness Habit Journal is to help you create happiness through positive habits that will bring you good feelings. You don't have to address all thirteen components of My Happiness Habit Journal every day. You should see them as a menu of happiness sources. You can choose the ones that work for you and then, if you want to, gradually add other components into your daily routine. The important thing is that you use My Happiness Habit Journal as a tool to help you take action to create happiness in your everyday life. Use it to help you make meaningful choices—of behavior, thoughts, words, and attitudes to boost *your* happiness.

Three

HOW TO USE MY HAPPINESS HABIT JOURNAL

After sharing the idea of My Happiness Habit Journal with other people, I heard comments such as, "This is a great idea! But people may not have the time to fill out the journal or practice all those habits every day"; "People have to be disciplined to do that"; and "This would work only for disciplined people." My reaction to those comments? Yes, disciplined people would find it easier to incorporate all the components of the journal into their lives and stick to them. However, it doesn't take more than ten minutes to fill out the journal. Besides, when filling it out, people don't have to address all the components or perform all the habits to benefit from My Happiness Habit Journal. People should consider this journal as a menu of happiness sources. They can choose the happiness sources that work for them.

My Happiness Habit Journal has the following components:

1. Happiness-source goals
2. Gratitudes
3. Circle of life
4. Happy moments
5. A conscious struggle
6. My commandments
7. Resolutions

8. Tiny habits
9. An accomplishment
10. An act of kindness
11. Spiritual master
12. Overall day rating
13. Happiness Trophy

I agree that thirteen components can be overwhelming, but you can combine some of them. For example, you can create a *tiny habit* to help you address a *resolution*. Say you have the *resolution* of *practicing the piano for fifteen minutes*. Then, your *tiny habit* can be, *"After I have dinner, I will practice the piano for fifteen minutes."* Or you can combine the *service goal* (from the circle of life) with *an act of kindness*. For instance, you can have, *"perform an act of kindness"* as your *service goal*. Combining the components will not only make the journal less overwhelming, but, more importantly, it will also reinforce the new habits.

I came up with three different ways to use My Happiness Habit Journal. I encourage you to choose the way that best fits you. You can also create your own way of using the journal; if you do it, please share it with me at: myhappinesshabitjournal@outlook.com.

Here are my suggestions for using My Happiness Habit Journal:

- Use it as a menu of happiness sources, meaning that you can choose the source(s) you want to focus on. For example, if you want to focus on gratitude, only fill out the happiness source *gratitude* in the journal.
- Start implementing only one happiness source at a time and gradually add new happiness sources into your routine. For instance, in the first week, you can focus on performing *an act of kindness* in your daily routine. Then, a week later, you can add writing down two *happy moments* to your routine, and so on.

- Fill out the first two components of My Happiness Habit Journal (*happiness-source goals* and *gratitudes*) in the morning and the other ones at night. (This is how I use the journal.)

No matter how you use My Happiness Habit Journal, it is essential that you personalize the journal for *you*. Different things make different people happy. So create *tiny habits*, *resolutions*, *commandments*, and *circle-of-life goals* based on *your* values, what matters to *you*, and what makes *you* happy.

Note: This journal is part of the book *Running into Happiness: How My Happiness Habit Journal Created Lasting Happiness in the Midst of a Crazy-busy Semester* by the author. In the book, I describe my happiness journey and explain the components of My Happiness Habit Journal in greater detail.

Four

SPIRITUAL MASTER

My spiritual master is

_____

Five

MY COMMANDMENTS

My commandments are

1. _____

2. _____

3. _____

4. _____

5. _____

6. _____

7. _____

8. _____

9. _____

10. _____

11. _____

12. _____

13. _____

14. _____

15. _____

Six

RESOLUTIONS

Resolutions

Days of the month	Resolutions				
	A	B	C	D	E
1					
2					
3					
4					
5					
6					
7					
8					
9					
10					
11					
12					
13					
14					
15					
16					
17					
18					
19					
20					
21					
22					
23					
24					
25					
26					
27					
28					
29					
30					
31					

Month

_____

Resolutions

A. _____

_____

_____

_____

B. _____

_____

_____

_____

C. _____

_____

_____

_____

D. _____

_____

_____

_____

E. _____

_____

_____

_____

Resolutions

Days of the month	Resolutions				
	A	B	C	D	E
1					
2					
3					
4					
5					
6					
7					
8					
9					
10					
11					
12					
13					
14					
15					
16					
17					
18					
19					
20					
21					
22					
23					
24					
25					
26					
27					
28					
29					
30					
31					

Month

_____

Resolutions

A. _____

_____

_____

_____

B. _____

_____

_____

_____

C. _____

_____

_____

_____

D. _____

_____

_____

_____

E. _____

_____

_____

_____

Resolutions

Days of the month	Resolutions				
	A	B	C	D	E
1					
2					
3					
4					
5					
6					
7					
8					
9					
10					
11					
12					
13					
14					
15					
16					
17					
18					
19					
20					
21					
22					
23					
24					
25					
26					
27					
28					
29					
30					
31					

Month

_____

Resolutions

A. _____

_____

_____

_____

B. _____

_____

_____

_____

C. _____

_____

_____

_____

D. _____

_____

_____

_____

E. _____

_____

_____

_____

Resolutions

Days of the month	Resolutions				
	A	B	C	D	E
1					
2					
3					
4					
5					
6					
7					
8					
9					
10					
11					
12					
13					
14					
15					
16					
17					
18					
19					
20					
21					
22					
23					
24					
25					
26					
27					
28					
29					
30					
31					

Month

_____

Resolutions

A. _____

_____

_____

_____

B. _____

_____

_____

_____

C. _____

_____

_____

_____

D. _____

_____

_____

_____

E. _____

_____

_____

_____

Resolutions

Days of the month	Resolutions				
	A	B	C	D	E
1					
2					
3					
4					
5					
6					
7					
8					
9					
10					
11					
12					
13					
14					
15					
16					
17					
18					
19					
20					
21					
22					
23					
24					
25					
26					
27					
28					
29					
30					
31					

Month

_____

Resolutions

A. _____

_____

_____

_____

B. _____

_____

_____

_____

C. _____

_____

_____

_____

D. _____

_____

_____

_____

E. _____

_____

_____

_____

Resolutions

Days of the month	Resolutions				
	A	B	C	D	E
1					
2					
3					
4					
5					
6					
7					
8					
9					
10					
11					
12					
13					
14					
15					
16					
17					
18					
19					
20					
21					
22					
23					
24					
25					
26					
27					
28					
29					
30					
31					

Month

_____

Resolutions

A. _____

_____

_____

_____

B. _____

_____

_____

_____

C. _____

_____

_____

_____

D. _____

_____

_____

_____

E. _____

_____

_____

_____

Seven

TINY HABITS

Tiny Habits

Days of the month	Tiny habits				
	A	B	C	D	E
1					
2					
3					
4					
5					
6					
7					
8					
9					
10					
11					
12					
13					
14					
15					
16					
17					
18					
19					
20					
21					
22					
23					
24					
25					
26					
27					
28					
29					
30					
31					

Month

_____

Tiny habits

A. *After I* _____

_____,

I will _____

_____.

B. *After I* _____

_____,

I will _____

_____.

C. *After I* _____

_____,

I will _____

_____.

D. *After I* _____

_____,

I will _____

_____.

E. *After I* _____

_____,

I will _____

_____.

Tiny Habits

Days of the month	Tiny habits				
	A	B	C	D	E
1					
2					
3					
4					
5					
6					
7					
8					
9					
10					
11					
12					
13					
14					
15					
16					
17					
18					
19					
20					
21					
22					
23					
24					
25					
26					
27					
28					
29					
30					
31					

Month

_____

Tiny habits

A. *After I* _____

_____,

I will _____

_____.

B. *After I* _____

_____,

I will _____

_____.

C. *After I* _____

_____,

I will _____

_____.

D. *After I* _____

_____,

I will _____

_____.

E. *After I* _____

_____,

I will _____

_____.

Tiny Habits

Days of the month	Tiny habits				
	A	B	C	D	E
1					
2					
3					
4					
5					
6					
7					
8					
9					
10					
11					
12					
13					
14					
15					
16					
17					
18					
19					
20					
21					
22					
23					
24					
25					
26					
27					
28					
29					
30					
31					

Month

_____

Tiny habits

A. *After I* _____

_____,

I will _____

_____.

B. *After I* _____

_____,

I will _____

_____.

C. *After I* _____

_____,

I will _____

_____.

D. *After I* _____

_____,

I will _____

_____.

E. *After I* _____

_____,

I will _____

_____.

Tiny Habits

Days of the month	Tiny habits					**Month**
	A	B	C	D	E	_____
1						
2						**Tiny habits**
3						
4						A. *After I* _____
5						
6						_____,
7						
8						*I will* _____
9						
10						_____.
11						
12						B. *After I* _____
13						
14						_____,
15						
16						*I will* _____
17						
18						_____.
19						
20						C. *After I* _____
21						
22						_____,
23						
24						*I will* _____
25						
26						_____.
27						
28						D. *After I* _____
29						
30						_____,
31						

I will _____

_____.

E. *After I* _____

_____,

I will _____

_____.

Tiny Habits

Days of the month	Tiny habits				
	A	B	C	D	E
1					
2					
3					
4					
5					
6					
7					
8					
9					
10					
11					
12					
13					
14					
15					
16					
17					
18					
19					
20					
21					
22					
23					
24					
25					
26					
27					
28					
29					
30					
31					

Month

_____

Tiny habits

A. *After I* _____

_____,

I will _____

_____.

B. *After I* _____

_____,

I will _____

_____.

C. *After I* _____

_____,

I will _____

_____.

D. *After I* _____

_____,

I will _____

_____.

E. *After I* _____

_____,

I will _____

_____.

Tiny Habits

Days of the month	Tiny habits				
	A	B	C	D	E
1					
2					
3					
4					
5					
6					
7					
8					
9					
10					
11					
12					
13					
14					
15					
16					
17					
18					
19					
20					
21					
22					
23					
24					
25					
26					
27					
28					
29					
30					
31					

Month

_____

Tiny habits

A. *After I* _____

_____,

I will _____

_____.

B. *After I* _____

_____,

I will _____

_____.

C. *After I* _____

_____,

I will _____

_____.

D. *After I* _____

_____,

I will _____

_____.

E. *After I* _____

_____,

I will _____

_____.

Eight

CIRCLE OF LIFE

Circle of Life

Days of the month	Circle-of-life goals									
	A	B	C	D	E	F	G	H	I	J
1										
2										
3										
4										
5										
6										
7										
8										
9										
10										
11										
12										
13										
14										
15										
16										
17										
18										
19										
20										
21										
22										
23										
24										
25										
26										
27										
28										
29										
30										
31										

Month

_____

Circle-of-life goals

A. *Health*: _____

_____

B. *Social*: _____

_____

C. *Relationship with a significant other*: _____

_____

_____

D. *Family*: _____

_____

E. *Spiritual*: _____

_____

F. *Emotional*: _____

_____

_____

G. *Professional*: _____

_____

H. *Financial*: _____

_____

_____

I. *Intellectual*: _____

_____

J. *Service*: _____

_____

_____

Circle of Life

Days of the month	Circle-of-life goals									
	A	B	C	D	E	F	G	H	I	J
1										
2										
3										
4										
5										
6										
7										
8										
9										
10										
11										
12										
13										
14										
15										
16										
17										
18										
19										
20										
21										
22										
23										
24										
25										
26										
27										
28										
29										
30										
31										

Month

_____

Circle-of-life goals

A. *Health*: _____

_____

B. *Social*: _____

_____

C. *Relationship with a significant other*: _____

_____

_____

D. *Family*: _____

_____

E. *Spiritual*: _____

_____

F. *Emotional*: _____

_____

_____

G. *Professional*: _____

_____

H. *Financial*: _____

_____

_____

I. *Intellectual*: _____

_____

J. *Service*: _____

_____

_____

Circle of Life

Days of the month	Circle-of-life goals									
	A	B	C	D	E	F	G	H	I	J
1										
2										
3										
4										
5										
6										
7										
8										
9										
10										
11										
12										
13										
14										
15										
16										
17										
18										
19										
20										
21										
22										
23										
24										
25										
26										
27										
28										
29										
30										
31										

Month

_____

Circle-of-life goals

A. *Health*: _____

_____

B. *Social*: _____

_____

C. *Relationship with a significant other*: _____

_____

_____

D. *Family*: _____

_____

E. *Spiritual*: _____

_____

F. *Emotional*: _____

_____

_____

G. *Professional*: _____

_____

H. *Financial*: _____

_____

_____

I. *Intellectual*: _____

_____

J. *Service*: _____

_____

_____

Circle of Life

Days of the month	Circle-of-life goals									
	A	B	C	D	E	F	G	H	I	J
1										
2										
3										
4										
5										
6										
7										
8										
9										
10										
11										
12										
13										
14										
15										
16										
17										
18										
19										
20										
21										
22										
23										
24										
25										
26										
27										
28										
29										
30										
31										

Month

_____

Circle-of-life goals

A. *Health*: _____

_____

B. *Social*: _____

_____

C. *Relationship with a significant other*: _____

_____

_____

D. *Family*: _____

_____

E. *Spiritual*: _____

_____

F. *Emotional*: _____

_____

_____

G. *Professional*: _____

_____

H. *Financial*: _____

_____

_____

I. *Intellectual*: _____

_____

J. *Service*: _____

_____

_____

Circle of Life

Days of the month	Circle-of-life goals									
	A	B	C	D	E	F	G	H	I	J
1										
2										
3										
4										
5										
6										
7										
8										
9										
10										
11										
12										
13										
14										
15										
16										
17										
18										
19										
20										
21										
22										
23										
24										
25										
26										
27										
28										
29										
30										
31										

Month

_____

Circle-of-life goals

A. *Health*: _____
_____

B. *Social*: _____
_____

C. *Relationship with a significant other*: _____
_____
_____

D. *Family*: _____
_____

E. *Spiritual*: _____
_____

F. *Emotional*: _____
_____
_____

G. *Professional*: _____
_____

H. *Financial*: _____
_____
_____

I. *Intellectual*: _____
_____

J. *Service*: _____
_____
_____

Circle of Life

Days of the month	Circle-of-life goals									
	A	B	C	D	E	F	G	H	I	J
1										
2										
3										
4										
5										
6										
7										
8										
9										
10										
11										
12										
13										
14										
15										
16										
17										
18										
19										
20										
21										
22										
23										
24										
25										
26										
27										
28										
29										
30										
31										

Month

_____

Circle-of-life goals

A. *Health*: _____

_____

B. *Social*: _____

_____

C. *Relationship with a significant other*: _____

_____

_____

D. *Family*: _____

_____

E. *Spiritual*: _____

_____

F. *Emotional*: _____

_____

_____

G. *Professional*: _____

_____

H. *Financial*: _____

_____

_____

I. *Intellectual*: _____

_____

J. *Service*: _____

_____

_____

Nine

DAILY JOURNAL

Part I: To be filled out in the morning   Date: _____ / _____ / _____

My **happiness-source goals** for today are...

Something **meaningful**	Something **pleasurable**
Something **challenging**	Something **unpleasurable**

I am **grateful** for...

+ _____

+ _____

+ _____

Part II: To be filled out at night

Two **happy moments** I had today were...

+ _____

+ _____

An **act of kindness** I did today was...

+ _____

_____

A **conscious struggle** I have is...

+ _____

_____

One **accomplishment** I had today was...

+ _____

My **Happiness Trophy** goes to:

+ _____

Overall my day was...

☺ ☺ ☹

Part I: To be filled out in the morning   Date: ____ / ____ / ____

My **happiness-source goals** for today are…

Something **meaningful**	Something **pleasurable**
Something **challenging**	Something **unpleasurable**

I am **grateful** for…

+ _____

+ _____

+ _____

Part II: To be filled out at night

Two **happy moments** I had today were…

+ _____

+ _____

_____

An **act of kindness** I did today was…

+ _____

_____

One **accomplishment** I had today was…

+ _____

A **conscious struggle** I have is…

+ _____

_____

_____

My **Happiness Trophy** goes to:

+ _____

Overall my day was...

☺ ☺ ☹

Part I: To be filled out in the morning   Date: ____ / ____ / ____

My **happiness-source goals** for today are...

Something **meaningful**	Something **pleasurable**
Something **challenging**	Something **unpleasurable**

I am **grateful** for...

✦ _____

✦ _____

✦ _____

Part II: To be filled out at night

Two **happy moments** I had today were...

✦ _____

_____

✦ _____

_____

An **act of kindness** I did today was...

✦ _____

_____

One **accomplishment** I had today was...

✦ _____

A **conscious struggle** I have is...

✦ _____

_____

_____

My **Happiness Trophy** goes to:

✦ _____

Overall my day was...

☺ 😐 ☹

Part I: To be filled out in the morning   Date: ____ / ____ / ____

My **happiness-source goals** for today are…

Something **meaningful**	Something **pleasurable**
Something **challenging**	Something **unpleasurable**

I am **grateful** for…

⚜ _____

⚜ _____

⚜ _____

Part II: To be filled out at night

Two **happy moments** I had today were…

⚜ _____

⚜ _____

_____

An **act of kindness** I did today was…

⚜ _____

_____

One **accomplishment** I had today was…

⚜ _____

A **conscious struggle** I have is…

⚜ _____

_____

_____

My **Happiness Trophy** goes to:

⚜ _____

Overall my day was…

☺ 😐 ☹

Part I: To be filled out in the morning   Date: ____ / ____ / ____

My **happiness-source goals** for today are…

Something **meaningful**	Something **pleasurable**
Something **challenging**	Something **unpleasurable**

I am **grateful** for…

+ _____
+ _____
+ _____

Part II: To be filled out at night

Two **happy moments** I had today were…

+ _____
+ _____

An **act of kindness** I did today was…

+ _____
  _____

One **accomplishment** I had today was…

+ _____

A **conscious struggle** I have is…

+ _____
  _____

My **Happiness Trophy** goes to:

+ _____

Overall my day was…

☺ 😐 ☹

Part I: To be filled out in the morning   Date: _____ / _____ / _____

My **happiness-source goals** for today are...

Something **meaningful**	Something **pleasurable**
Something **challenging**	Something **unpleasurable**

I am **grateful** for...

⚓ _____

⚓ _____

⚓ _____

Part II: To be filled out at night

Two **happy moments** I had today were...

⚓ _____

⚓ _____
_____

An **act of kindness** I did today was...

⚓ _____
_____

One **accomplishment** I had today was...

⚓ _____

A **conscious struggle** I have is...

⚓ _____
_____
_____

My **Happiness Trophy** goes to:

⚓ _____

Overall my day was...

☺ 😐 ☹

Part I: To be filled out in the morning   Date: ____ / ____ / ____

My **happiness-source goals** for today are…

Something **meaningful**	Something **pleasurable**
Something **challenging**	Something **unpleasurable**

I am **grateful** for…

+ _____

+ _____

+ _____

Part II: To be filled out at night

Two **happy moments** I had today were…

+ _____

+ _____

An **act of kindness** I did today was…

+ _____

_____

One **accomplishment** I had today was…

+ _____

A **conscious struggle** I have is…

+ _____

_____

My **Happiness Trophy** goes to:

+ _____

Overall my day was…

☺ ☺ ☹

Part I: To be filled out in the morning   Date: ____ / ____ / ____

My **happiness-source goals** for today are...

Something **meaningful**	Something **pleasurable**
Something **challenging**	Something **unpleasurable**

I am **grateful** for...

+ _____

+ _____

+ _____

Part II: To be filled out at night

Two **happy moments** I had today were...

+ _____

+ _____
_____

An **act of kindness** I did today was...

+ _____
_____

One **accomplishment** I had today was...

+ _____

A **conscious struggle** I have is...

+ _____
_____
_____

My **Happiness Trophy** goes to:

+ _____

Overall my day was...

☺ 😐 ☹

Part I: To be filled out in the morning   Date: ____ / ____ / ____

My **happiness-source goals** for today are…

Something **meaningful**	Something **pleasurable**
Something **challenging**	Something **unpleasurable**

I am **grateful** for…

✦ _____

✦ _____

✦ _____

Part II: To be filled out at night

Two **happy moments** I had today were…

✦ _____

✦ _____

_____

An **act of kindness** I did today was…

✦ _____

_____

One **accomplishment** I had today was…

✦ _____

A **conscious struggle** I have is…

✦ _____

_____

My **Happiness Trophy** goes to:

✦ _____

Overall my day was…

☺ 😐 ☹

Part I: To be filled out in the morning   Date: ____ / ____ / ____

My **happiness-source goals** for today are...

Something **meaningful**	Something **pleasurable**
Something **challenging**	Something **unpleasurable**

I am **grateful** for...

✦ _____

✦ _____

✦ _____

Part II: To be filled out at night

Two **happy moments** I had today were...

✦ _____

✦ _____

_____

An **act of kindness** I did today was...

✦ _____

_____

One **accomplishment** I had today was...

✦ _____

A **conscious struggle** I have is...

✦ _____

_____

_____

My **Happiness Trophy** goes to:

✦ _____

Overall my day was...

☺ 😐 ☹

Part I: To be filled out in the morning   Date: _____ / _____ / _____

My **happiness-source goals** for today are…

Something **meaningful**	Something **pleasurable**
Something **challenging**	Something **unpleasurable**

I am **grateful** for…

+ _____

+ _____

+ _____

Part II: To be filled out at night

Two **happy moments** I had today were…

+ _____

+ _____

_____

One **accomplishment** I had today was…

+ _____

My **Happiness Trophy** goes to:

+ _____

An **act of kindness** I did today was…

+ _____

_____

A **conscious struggle** I have is…

+ _____

_____

_____

Overall my day was…

☺ ☺ ☹

Part I: To be filled out in the morning   Date: ____ / ____ /____

My **happiness-source goals** for today are…

Something **meaningful**	Something **pleasurable**
Something **challenging**	Something **unpleasurable**

I am **grateful** for…

+ _____

+ _____

+ _____

Part II: To be filled out at night

Two **happy moments** I had today were…

+ _____

+ _____

_____

An **act of kindness** I did today was…

+ _____

_____

One **accomplishment** I had today was…

+ _____

A **conscious struggle** I have is…

+ _____

_____

My **Happiness Trophy** goes to:

+ _____

Overall my day was…

☺ ☹ ☹

Part I: To be filled out in the morning   Date: ____ / ____ / ____

My **happiness-source goals** for today are…

Something **meaningful**	Something **pleasurable**
Something **challenging**	Something **unpleasurable**

I am **grateful** for…

+ _____
+ _____
+ _____

Part II: To be filled out at night

Two **happy moments** I had today were…

+ _____
+ _____
  _____

An **act of kindness** I did today was…

+ _____
  _____

One **accomplishment** I had today was…

+ _____

A **conscious struggle** I have is…

+ _____
  _____

My **Happiness Trophy** goes to:

+ _____

Overall my day was...

☺ ☺ ☹

Part I: To be filled out in the morning   Date: ____ / ____ / ____

My **happiness-source goals** for today are...

Something **meaningful**	Something **pleasurable**
Something **challenging**	Something **unpleasurable**

I am **grateful** for...

🙣 _____

🙣 _____

🙣 _____

Part II: To be filled out at night

Two **happy moments** I had today were...

🙣 _____

🙣 _____

_____

An **act of kindness** I did today was...

🙣 _____

_____

One **accomplishment** I had today was...

🙣 _____

A **conscious struggle** I have is...

🙣 _____

_____

_____

My **Happiness Trophy** goes to:

🙣 _____

Overall my day was...

☺ 😐 ☹

Part I: To be filled out in the morning   Date: ___ / ___ / ___

My **happiness-source goals** for today are…

Something **meaningful**	Something **pleasurable**
Something **challenging**	Something **unpleasurable**

I am **grateful** for…

✦ _____

✦ _____

✦ _____

Part II: To be filled out at night

Two **happy moments** I had today were…

✦ _____

✦ _____

_____

An **act of kindness** I did today was…

✦ _____

_____

One **accomplishment** I had today was…

✦ _____

A **conscious struggle** I have is…

✦ _____

_____

_____

My **Happiness Trophy** goes to:

✦ _____

Overall my day was…

☺ 😐 ☹

Part I: To be filled out in the morning   Date: ____ / ____ / ____

My **happiness-source goals** for today are…

Something **meaningful**	Something **pleasurable**
Something **challenging**	Something **unpleasurable**

I am **grateful** for…

+ _____

+ _____

+ _____

Part II: To be filled out at night

Two **happy moments** I had today were…

+ _____

+ _____

An **act of kindness** I did today was…

+ _____

A **conscious struggle** I have is…

+ _____

One **accomplishment** I had today was…

+ _____

My **Happiness Trophy** goes to:

+ _____

Overall my day was…

☺ ☺ ☹

Part I: To be filled out in the morning   Date: ____ / ____ / ____

My **happiness-source goals** for today are…

Something **meaningful**	Something **pleasurable**
Something **challenging**	Something **unpleasurable**

I am **grateful** for…

✦ _____

✦ _____

✦ _____

Part II: To be filled out at night

Two **happy moments** I had today were…

✦ _____

✦ _____

An **act of kindness** I did today was…

✦ _____

_____

One **accomplishment** I had today was…

✦ _____

A **conscious struggle** I have is…

✦ _____

_____

My **Happiness Trophy** goes to:

✦ _____

Overall my day was…

☺ 😐 ☹

Part I: To be filled out in the morning   Date: ____ / ____ / ____

My **happiness-source goals** for today are…

Something **meaningful**	Something **pleasurable**
Something **challenging**	Something **unpleasurable**

I am **grateful** for…

+ _____
+ _____
+ _____

Part II: To be filled out at night

Two **happy moments** I had today were…
+ _____
+ _____
  _____

One **accomplishment** I had today was…
+ _____

My **Happiness Trophy** goes to:
+ _____

An **act of kindness** I did today was…
+ _____
  _____

A **conscious struggle** I have is…
+ _____
  _____

Overall my day was…

☺ ☺ ☹

Part I: To be filled out in the morning   Date: _____ / _____ / _____

My **happiness-source goals** for today are…

Something **meaningful**	Something **pleasurable**
Something **challenging**	Something **unpleasurable**

I am **grateful** for…

✦ _____

✦ _____

✦ _____

Part II: To be filled out at night

Two **happy moments** I had today were…

✦ _____

✦ _____

_____

An **act of kindness** I did today was…

✦ _____

_____

One **accomplishment** I had today was…

✦ _____

A **conscious struggle** I have is…

✦ _____

_____

_____

My **Happiness Trophy** goes to:

✦ _____

Overall my day was…

☺ ☻ ☹

Part I: To be filled out in the morning   Date: ____ / ____ / ____

My **happiness-source goals** for today are...

Something **meaningful**	Something **pleasurable**
Something **challenging**	Something **unpleasurable**

I am **grateful** for...

✦ _____

✦ _____

✦ _____

Part II: To be filled out at night

Two **happy moments** I had today were...

✦ _____

✦ _____

_____

One **accomplishment** I had today was...

✦ _____

My **Happiness Trophy** goes to:

✦ _____

An **act of kindness** I did today was...

✦ _____

_____

A **conscious struggle** I have is...

✦ _____

_____

_____

Overall my day was...

☺ ☺ ☹

Part I: To be filled out in the morning   Date: _____ / _____ / _____

My **happiness-source goals** for today are...

Something **meaningful**	Something **pleasurable**
Something **challenging**	Something **unpleasurable**

I am **grateful** for...

➤ _____

➤ _____

➤ _____

Part II: To be filled out at night

Two **happy moments** I had today were...

➤ _____

➤ _____

_____

One **accomplishment** I had today was...

➤ _____

My **Happiness Trophy** goes to:

➤ _____

An **act of kindness** I did today was...

➤ _____

_____

A **conscious struggle** I have is...

➤ _____

_____

Overall my day was...

☺ ☺ ☹

Part I: To be filled out in the morning   Date: _____ / _____ / _____

My **happiness-source goals** for today are...

Something **meaningful**	Something **pleasurable**
Something **challenging**	Something **unpleasurable**

I am **grateful** for...

✦ _____

✦ _____

✦ _____

Part II: To be filled out at night

Two **happy moments** I had today were...

✦ _____

✦ _____

An **act of kindness** I did today was...

✦ _____

_____

One **accomplishment** I had today was...

✦ _____

A **conscious struggle** I have is...

✦ _____

_____

_____

My **Happiness Trophy** goes to:

✦ _____

Overall my day was...

☺ 😐 ☹

Part I: To be filled out in the morning   Date: ____ / ____ / ____

My **happiness-source goals** for today are...

Something **meaningful**	Something **pleasurable**
Something **challenging**	Something **unpleasurable**

I am **grateful** for...

✦ _____

✦ _____

✦ _____

Part II: To be filled out at night

Two **happy moments** I had today were...

✦ _____

✦ _____
  _____

One **accomplishment** I had today was...

✦ _____

My **Happiness Trophy** goes to:

✦ _____

An **act of kindness** I did today was...

✦ _____
  _____

A **conscious struggle** I have is...

✦ _____
  _____
  _____

Overall my day was...

☺ 😐 ☹

Part I: To be filled out in the morning   Date: _____ / _____ / _____

My **happiness-source goals** for today are...

Something **meaningful**	Something **pleasurable**
Something **challenging**	Something **unpleasurable**

I am **grateful** for...

✦ _____

✦ _____

✦ _____

Part II: To be filled out at night

Two **happy moments** I had today were...

✦ _____

✦ _____

One **accomplishment** I had today was...

✦ _____

My **Happiness Trophy** goes to:

✦ _____

An **act of kindness** I did today was...

✦ _____

A **conscious struggle** I have is...

✦ _____

Overall my day was...

☺ ☺ ☹

Part I: To be filled out in the morning   Date: _____ / _____ / _____

My **happiness-source goals** for today are…

Something **meaningful**	Something **pleasurable**
Something **challenging**	Something **unpleasurable**

I am **grateful** for…

+ _____

+ _____

+ _____

Part II: To be filled out at night

Two **happy moments** I had today were…

+ _____

+ _____
 _____

An **act of kindness** I did today was…

+ _____
 _____

One **accomplishment** I had today was…

+ _____

A **conscious struggle** I have is…

+ _____
 _____
 _____

My **Happiness Trophy** goes to:

+ _____

Overall my day was…

☺ 😐 ☹

Part I: To be filled out in the morning   Date: ____ / ____ / ____

My **happiness-source goals** for today are...

Something **meaningful**	Something **pleasurable**
Something **challenging**	Something **unpleasurable**

I am **grateful** for...

+ _____

+ _____

+ _____

Part II: To be filled out at night

Two **happy moments** I had today were...

+ _____

+ _____

An **act of kindness** I did today was...

+ _____

_____

One **accomplishment** I had today was...

+ _____

A **conscious struggle** I have is...

+ _____

_____

My **Happiness Trophy** goes to:

+ _____

Overall my day was...

☺ ☺ ☹

Part I: To be filled out in the morning   Date: _____ / _____ / _____

My **happiness-source goals** for today are…

Something **meaningful**	Something **pleasurable**
Something **challenging**	Something **unpleasurable**

I am **grateful** for…

+ _____

+ _____

+ _____

Part II: To be filled out at night

Two **happy moments** I had today were…

+ _____

+ _____

_____

One **accomplishment** I had today was…

+ _____

My **Happiness Trophy** goes to:

+ _____

An **act of kindness** I did today was…

+ _____

_____

A **conscious struggle** I have is…

+ _____

_____

_____

Overall my day was...

☺ ☺ ☹

Part I: To be filled out in the morning   Date: ____ / ____ / ____

My **happiness-source goals** for today are...

Something **meaningful**	Something **pleasurable**
Something **challenging**	Something **unpleasurable**

I am **grateful** for...

🍂 _____

🍂 _____

🍂 _____

Part II: To be filled out at night

Two **happy moments** I had today were...

🍂 _____

_____

🍂 _____

_____

An **act of kindness** I did today was...

🍂 _____

_____

One **accomplishment** I had today was...

🍂 _____

A **conscious struggle** I have is...

🍂 _____

_____

_____

My **Happiness Trophy** goes to:

🍂 _____

Overall my day was...

☺ 😐 ☹

Part I: To be filled out in the morning   Date: _____ / _____ / _____

My **happiness-source goals** for today are…

Something **meaningful**	Something **pleasurable**
Something **challenging**	Something **unpleasurable**

I am **grateful** for…

+ _____

+ _____

+ _____

Part II: To be filled out at night

Two **happy moments** I had today were…

+ _____

+ _____

_____

One **accomplishment** I had today was…

+ _____

My **Happiness Trophy** goes to:

+ _____

An **act of kindness** I did today was…

+ _____

_____

A **conscious struggle** I have is…

+ _____

_____

_____

Overall my day was...

☺ ☺ ☹

Part I: To be filled out in the morning   Date: ____ / ____ / ____

My **happiness-source goals** for today are...

Something **meaningful**	Something **pleasurable**
Something **challenging**	Something **unpleasurable**

I am **grateful** for...

🕂 _____

🕂 _____

🕂 _____

Part II: To be filled out at night

Two **happy moments** I had today were...

🕂 _____

🕂 _____

_____

An **act of kindness** I did today was...

🕂 _____

_____

A **conscious struggle** I have is...

🕂 _____

_____

_____

One **accomplishment** I had today was...

🕂 _____

My **Happiness Trophy** goes to:

🕂 _____

Overall my day was...

☺ 😐 ☹

Part I: To be filled out in the morning   Date: ____ / ____ / ____

My **happiness-source goals** for today are...

Something **meaningful**	Something **pleasurable**
Something **challenging**	Something **unpleasurable**

I am **grateful** for...

+ _____

+ _____

+ _____

Part II: To be filled out at night

Two **happy moments** I had today were...

+ _____

+ _____

_____

One **accomplishment** I had today was...

+ _____

My **Happiness Trophy** goes to:

+ _____

An **act of kindness** I did today was...

+ _____

_____

A **conscious struggle** I have is...

+ _____

_____

_____

Overall my day was...

☺ ☺ ☹

Part I: To be filled out in the morning Date: ____ / ____ / ____

My **happiness-source goals** for today are...

Something **meaningful**	Something **pleasurable**
Something **challenging**	Something **unpleasurable**

I am **grateful** for...

⚜ _____

⚜ _____

⚜ _____

Part II: To be filled out at night

Two **happy moments** I had today were...

⚜ _____

⚜ _____

An **act of kindness** I did today was...

⚜ _____

_____

One **accomplishment** I had today was...

⚜ _____

A **conscious struggle** I have is...

⚜ _____

_____

_____

My **Happiness Trophy** goes to:

⚜ _____

Overall my day was...

☺ 😐 ☹

Part I: To be filled out in the morning   Date: ____ / ____ / ____

My **happiness-source goals** for today are...

Something **meaningful**	Something **pleasurable**
Something **challenging**	Something **unpleasurable**

I am **grateful** for...

⁂ _____

⁂ _____

⁂ _____

Part II: To be filled out at night

Two **happy moments** I had today were...

⁂ _____

⁂ _____

An **act of kindness** I did today was...

⁂ _____

_____

One **accomplishment** I had today was...

⁂ _____

A **conscious struggle** I have is...

⁂ _____

_____

_____

My **Happiness Trophy** goes to:

⁂ _____

Overall my day was...

☺ ☺ ☹

Part I: To be filled out in the morning   Date: _____ / _____ / _____

My **happiness-source goals** for today are...

Something **meaningful**	Something **pleasurable**
Something **challenging**	Something **unpleasurable**

I am **grateful** for...

+ _____
+ _____
+ _____

Part II: To be filled out at night

Two **happy moments** I had today were...

+ _____
+ _____

An **act of kindness** I did today was...

+ _____
_____

One **accomplishment** I had today was...

+ _____

A **conscious struggle** I have is...

+ _____
_____
_____

My **Happiness Trophy** goes to:

+ _____

Overall my day was...

☺ ☺ ☹

Part I: To be filled out in the morning   Date: ____ / ____ / ____

My **happiness-source goals** for today are…

Something **meaningful**	Something **pleasurable**
Something **challenging**	Something **unpleasurable**

I am **grateful** for…

+ _____

+ _____

+ _____

Part II: To be filled out at night

Two **happy moments** I had today were…

+ _____

+ _____
_____

An **act of kindness** I did today was…

+ _____
_____

One **accomplishment** I had today was…

+ _____

A **conscious struggle** I have is…

+ _____
_____
_____

My **Happiness Trophy** goes to:

+ _____

Overall my day was...

☺ ☺ ☹

Part I: To be filled out in the morning   Date: _____ / _____ / _____

My **happiness-source goals** for today are…

Something **meaningful**	Something **pleasurable**
Something **challenging**	Something **unpleasurable**

I am **grateful** for…

✦ _____

✦ _____

✦ _____

Part II: To be filled out at night

Two **happy moments** I had today were…

✦ _____

✦ _____

One **accomplishment** I had today was…

✦ _____

My **Happiness Trophy** goes to:

✦ _____

An **act of kindness** I did today was…

✦ _____

A **conscious struggle** I have is…

✦ _____

Overall my day was…

☺ ☺ ☹

Part I: To be filled out in the morning   Date: _____ / _____ / _____

My **happiness-source goals** for today are…

Something **meaningful**	Something **pleasurable**
Something **challenging**	Something **unpleasurable**

I am **grateful** for…

+ _____

+ _____

+ _____

Part II: To be filled out at night

Two **happy moments** I had today were…

+ _____

+ _____

An **act of kindness** I did today was…

+ _____

One **accomplishment** I had today was…

+ _____

A **conscious struggle** I have is…

+ _____

My **Happiness Trophy** goes to:

+ _____

Overall my day was...

☺ ☺ ☹

Part I: To be filled out in the morning   Date: _____ / _____ / _____

My **happiness-source goals** for today are…

Something **meaningful**	Something **pleasurable**
Something **challenging**	Something **unpleasurable**

I am **grateful** for…

+ _____

+ _____

+ _____

Part II: To be filled out at night

Two **happy moments** I had today were…

+ _____

+ _____

An **act of kindness** I did today was…

+ _____

_____

One **accomplishment** I had today was…

+ _____

A **conscious struggle** I have is…

+ _____

_____

_____

My **Happiness Trophy** goes to:

+ _____

Overall my day was…

☺ ☺ ☹

Part I: To be filled out in the morning   Date: ____ / ____ / ____

My **happiness-source goals** for today are…

Something **meaningful**	Something **pleasurable**
Something **challenging**	Something **unpleasurable**

I am **grateful** for…

+ _____

+ _____

+ _____

Part II: To be filled out at night

Two **happy moments** I had today were…

+ _____

+ _____

_____

An **act of kindness** I did today was…

+ _____

_____

A **conscious struggle** I have is…

+ _____

_____

_____

One **accomplishment** I had today was…

+ _____

My **Happiness Trophy** goes to:

+ _____

Overall my day was…

☺ ☺ ☹

Part I: To be filled out in the morning   Date: _____ / _____ / _____

My **happiness-source goals** for today are...

Something **meaningful**	Something **pleasurable**
Something **challenging**	Something **unpleasurable**

I am **grateful** for...

+ _____

+ _____

+ _____

Part II: To be filled out at night

Two **happy moments** I had today were...

+ _____

+ _____

_____

An **act of kindness** I did today was...

+ _____

_____

One **accomplishment** I had today was...

+ _____

A **conscious struggle** I have is...

+ _____

_____

_____

My **Happiness Trophy** goes to:

+ _____

Overall my day was...

☺ ☺ ☹

Part I: To be filled out in the morning   Date: ____ / ____ / ____

My **happiness-source goals** for today are...

Something **meaningful**	Something **pleasurable**
Something **challenging**	Something **unpleasurable**

I am **grateful** for...

- _____
- _____
- _____

Part II: To be filled out at night

Two **happy moments** I had today were...
- _____
- _____
  _____

An **act of kindness** I did today was...
- _____
  _____

One **accomplishment** I had today was...
- _____

A **conscious struggle** I have is...
- _____
  _____
  _____

My **Happiness Trophy** goes to:
- _____

Overall my day was...

☺ ☺ ☹

Part I: To be filled out in the morning   Date: ____ / ____ /____

My **happiness-source goals** for today are…

Something **meaningful**	Something **pleasurable**
Something **challenging**	Something **unpleasurable**

I am **grateful** for…

⚜ _____

⚜ _____

⚜ _____

Part II: To be filled out at night

Two **happy moments** I had today were…

⚜ _____

⚜ _____

_____

An **act of kindness** I did today was…

⚜ _____

_____

One **accomplishment** I had today was…

⚜ _____

A **conscious struggle** I have is…

⚜ _____

_____

_____

My **Happiness Trophy** goes to:

⚜ _____

Overall my day was…

☺ ☺ ☹

Part I: To be filled out in the morning   Date: ____ / ____ / ____

My **happiness-source goals** for today are…

Something **meaningful**	Something **pleasurable**
Something **challenging**	Something **unpleasurable**

I am **grateful** for…

✦ _____

✦ _____

✦ _____

Part II: To be filled out at night

Two **happy moments** I had today were…

✦ _____

✦ _____

An **act of kindness** I did today was…

✦ _____

_____

One **accomplishment** I had today was…

✦ _____

A **conscious struggle** I have is…

✦ _____

_____

_____

My **Happiness Trophy** goes to:

✦ _____

Overall my day was…

☺ 😐 ☹

Part I: To be filled out in the morning   Date: ____ / ____ / ____

My **happiness-source goals** for today are…

Something **meaningful**	Something **pleasurable**
Something **challenging**	Something **unpleasurable**

I am **grateful** for…

+ _____

+ _____

+ _____

Part II: To be filled out at night

Two **happy moments** I had today were…

+ _____

+ _____

An **act of kindness** I did today was…

+ _____

A **conscious struggle** I have is…

+ _____

One **accomplishment** I had today was…

+ _____

My **Happiness Trophy** goes to:

+ _____

Overall my day was…

☺ ☺ ☹

Part I: To be filled out in the morning   Date: ____ / ____ / ____

My **happiness-source goals** for today are...

Something **meaningful**	Something **pleasurable**
Something **challenging**	Something **unpleasurable**

I am **grateful** for...

⚜ _____

⚜ _____

⚜ _____

Part II: To be filled out at night

Two **happy moments** I had today were...

⚜ _____

⚜ _____

_____

One **accomplishment** I had today was...

⚜ _____

My **Happiness Trophy** goes to:

⚜ _____

An **act of kindness** I did today was...

⚜ _____

_____

A **conscious struggle** I have is...

⚜ _____

_____

_____

Overall my day was...

☺ ☻ ☹

Part I: To be filled out in the morning   Date: _____ / _____ / _____

My **happiness-source goals** for today are...

Something **meaningful**	Something **pleasurable**
Something **challenging**	Something **unpleasurable**

I am **grateful** for...

⚜ _____

⚜ _____

⚜ _____

Part II: To be filled out at night

Two **happy moments** I had today were...

⚜ _____

⚜ _____

_____

An **act of kindness** I did today was...

⚜ _____

_____

One **accomplishment** I had today was...

⚜ _____

A **conscious struggle** I have is...

⚜ _____

_____

_____

My **Happiness Trophy** goes to:

⚜ _____

Overall my day was...

☺ 😐 ☹

Part I: To be filled out in the morning   Date: ____ / ____ / ____

My **happiness-source goals** for today are...

Something **meaningful**	Something **pleasurable**
Something **challenging**	Something **unpleasurable**

I am **grateful** for...

+ _____

+ _____

+ _____

Part II: To be filled out at night

Two **happy moments** I had today were...

+ _____

+ _____

_____

An **act of kindness** I did today was...

+ _____

_____

One **accomplishment** I had today was...

+ _____

A **conscious struggle** I have is...

+ _____

_____

_____

My **Happiness Trophy** goes to:

+ _____

Overall my day was...

☺ ☺ ☹

Part I: To be filled out in the morning   Date: ____ / ____ /____

My **happiness-source goals** for today are…

Something **meaningful**	Something **pleasurable**
Something **challenging**	Something **unpleasurable**

I am **grateful** for…

+ _____

+ _____

+ _____

Part II: To be filled out at night

Two **happy moments** I had today were…

+ _____

+ _____

_____

An **act of kindness** I did today was…

+ _____

_____

One **accomplishment** I had today was…

+ _____

A **conscious struggle** I have is…

+ _____

_____

_____

My **Happiness Trophy** goes to:

+ _____

Overall my day was…

☺ ☹ ☹

Part I: To be filled out in the morning   Date: ____ / ____ / ____

My **happiness-source goals** for today are…

Something **meaningful**	Something **pleasurable**
Something **challenging**	Something **unpleasurable**

I am **grateful** for…

* _____
* _____
* _____

Part II: To be filled out at night

Two **happy moments** I had today were…

* _____
* _____
_____

An **act of kindness** I did today was…

* _____
_____

One **accomplishment** I had today was…

* _____

A **conscious struggle** I have is…

* _____
_____
_____

My **Happiness Trophy** goes to:

* _____

Overall my day was…

☺ 😐 ☹

Part I: To be filled out in the morning   Date: _____ / _____ / _____

My **happiness-source goals** for today are...

Something **meaningful**	Something **pleasurable**
Something **challenging**	Something **unpleasurable**

I am **grateful** for...

+ _____

+ _____

+ _____

Part II: To be filled out at night

Two **happy moments** I had today were...

+ _____

+ _____

An **act of kindness** I did today was...

+ _____

A **conscious struggle** I have is...

+ _____

One **accomplishment** I had today was...

+ _____

My **Happiness Trophy** goes to:

+ _____

Overall my day was...

☺ ☺ ☹

Part I: To be filled out in the morning   Date: _____ / _____ / _____

My **happiness-source goals** for today are…

Something **meaningful**	Something **pleasurable**
Something **challenging**	Something **unpleasurable**

I am **grateful** for…

+ _____

+ _____

+ _____

Part II: To be filled out at night

Two **happy moments** I had today were…

+ _____

+ _____

_____

An **act of kindness** I did today was…

+ _____

_____

One **accomplishment** I had today was…

+ _____

A **conscious struggle** I have is…

+ _____

_____

_____

My **Happiness Trophy** goes to:

+ _____

Overall my day was...

☺ ☺ ☹

Part I: To be filled out in the morning   Date: _____ / _____ /_____

My **happiness-source goals** for today are...

Something **meaningful**	Something **pleasurable**
Something **challenging**	Something **unpleasurable**

I am **grateful** for...

+ _____

+ _____

+ _____

Part II: To be filled out at night

Two **happy moments** I had today were...

+ _____

+ _____

An **act of kindness** I did today was...

+ _____

A **conscious struggle** I have is...

+ _____

One **accomplishment** I had today was...

+ _____

My **Happiness Trophy** goes to:

+ _____

Overall my day was...

☺ ☺ ☹

Part I: To be filled out in the morning   Date: ____ / ____ / ____

My **happiness-source goals** for today are…

Something **meaningful**	Something **pleasurable**
Something **challenging**	Something **unpleasurable**

I am **grateful** for…

- _____
- _____
- _____

Part II: To be filled out at night

Two **happy moments** I had today were…
- _____
- _____
_____

An **act of kindness** I did today was…
- _____
_____

One **accomplishment** I had today was…
- _____

A **conscious struggle** I have is…
- _____
_____
_____

My **Happiness Trophy** goes to:
- _____

Overall my day was…

☺ 😐 ☹

Part I: To be filled out in the morning   Date: ____ / ____ / ____

My **happiness-source goals** for today are…

Something **meaningful**	Something **pleasurable**
Something **challenging**	Something **unpleasurable**

I am **grateful** for…

+ _____

+ _____

+ _____

Part II: To be filled out at night

Two **happy moments** I had today were…

+ _____
  _____

+ _____
  _____

An **act of kindness** I did today was…

+ _____
  _____

One **accomplishment** I had today was…

+ _____

A **conscious struggle** I have is…

+ _____
  _____
  _____

My **Happiness Trophy** goes to:

+ _____

Overall my day was…

☺ 😐 ☹

Part I: To be filled out in the morning Date: ____ / ____ / ____

My **happiness-source goals** for today are…

Something **meaningful**	Something **pleasurable**
Something **challenging**	Something **unpleasurable**

I am **grateful** for…

⊹ _____

⊹ _____

⊹ _____

Part II: To be filled out at night

Two **happy moments** I had today were…

⊹ _____

⊹ _____

_____

An **act of kindness** I did today was…

⊹ _____

_____

One **accomplishment** I had today was…

⊹ _____

A **conscious struggle** I have is…

⊹ _____

_____

_____

My **Happiness Trophy** goes to:

⊹ _____

Overall my day was…

☺ ☺ ☹

Part I: To be filled out in the morning   Date: ____ / ____ / ____

My **happiness-source goals** for today are…

Something **meaningful**	Something **pleasurable**
Something **challenging**	Something **unpleasurable**

I am **grateful** for…

⚜ _____

⚜ _____

⚜ _____

Part II: To be filled out at night

Two **happy moments** I had today were…

⚜ _____

⚜ _____

_____

An **act of kindness** I did today was…

⚜ _____

_____

One **accomplishment** I had today was…

⚜ _____

A **conscious struggle** I have is…

⚜ _____

_____

_____

My **Happiness Trophy** goes to:

⚜ _____

Overall my day was…

☺ ☺ ☹

Part I: To be filled out in the morning   Date: ____ / ____ / ____

My **happiness-source goals** for today are...

Something **meaningful**	Something **pleasurable**
Something **challenging**	Something **unpleasurable**

I am **grateful** for...

_____

_____

_____

Part II: To be filled out at night

Two **happy moments** I had today were...

- _____
- _____
- _____

An **act of kindness** I did today was...

- _____
- _____

One **accomplishment** I had today was...

- _____

A **conscious struggle** I have is...

- _____
- _____
- _____

My **Happiness Trophy** goes to:

- _____

Overall my day was...

☺ 😐 ☹

Part I: To be filled out in the morning   Date: ____ / ____ / ____

My **happiness-source goals** for today are...

Something **meaningful**	Something **pleasurable**
Something **challenging**	Something **unpleasurable**

I am **grateful** for...

⚜ _____

⚜ _____

⚜ _____

Part II: To be filled out at night

Two **happy moments** I had today were...

⚜ _____

⚜ _____

_____

An **act of kindness** I did today was...

⚜ _____

_____

A **conscious struggle** I have is...

⚜ _____

_____

_____

One **accomplishment** I had today was...

⚜ _____

My **Happiness Trophy** goes to:

⚜ _____

Overall my day was...

☺ 😐 ☹

Part I: To be filled out in the morning   Date: ____ / ____ / ____

My **happiness-source goals** for today are...

Something **meaningful**	Something **pleasurable**
Something **challenging**	Something **unpleasurable**

I am **grateful** for...

+ _____

+ _____

+ _____

Part II: To be filled out at night

Two **happy moments** I had today were...

+ _____

+ _____

+ _____

An **act of kindness** I did today was...

+ _____

_____

One **accomplishment** I had today was...

+ _____

A **conscious struggle** I have is...

+ _____

_____

_____

My **Happiness Trophy** goes to:

+ _____

Overall my day was...

☺ ☻ ☹

Part I: To be filled out in the morning   Date: ____ / ____ / ____

My **happiness-source goals** for today are...

Something **meaningful**	Something **pleasurable**
Something **challenging**	Something **unpleasurable**

I am **grateful** for...

+ _____

+ _____

+ _____

Part II: To be filled out at night

Two **happy moments** I had today were...

+ _____

+ _____

_____

An **act of kindness** I did today was...

+ _____

_____

One **accomplishment** I had today was...

+ _____

A **conscious struggle** I have is...

+ _____

_____

_____

My **Happiness Trophy** goes to:

+ _____

Overall my day was...

☺ 😐 ☹

Part I: To be filled out in the morning   Date: ____ / ____ / ____

My **happiness-source goals** for today are...

Something **meaningful**	Something **pleasurable**
Something **challenging**	Something **unpleasurable**

I am **grateful** for...

+ _____

+ _____

+ _____

Part II: To be filled out at night

Two **happy moments** I had today were...

+ _____

+ _____

_____

One **accomplishment** I had today was...

+ _____

My **Happiness Trophy** goes to:

+ _____

An **act of kindness** I did today was...

+ _____

_____

A **conscious struggle** I have is...

+ _____

_____

_____

Overall my day was...

☺ ☺ ☹

Part I: To be filled out in the morning   Date: ____ / ____ / ____

My **happiness-source goals** for today are…

Something **meaningful**	Something **pleasurable**
Something **challenging**	Something **unpleasurable**

I am **grateful** for…

🕏 _____

🕏 _____

🕏 _____

Part II: To be filled out at night

Two **happy moments** I had today were…

🕏 _____

🕏 _____

_____

An **act of kindness** I did today was…

🕏 _____

_____

One **accomplishment** I had today was…

🕏 _____

A **conscious struggle** I have is…

🕏 _____

_____

_____

My **Happiness Trophy** goes to:

🕏 _____

Overall my day was…

☺ 😐 ☹

Part I: To be filled out in the morning   Date: ____ / ____ / ____

My **happiness-source goals** for today are...

Something **meaningful**	Something **pleasurable**
Something **challenging**	Something **unpleasurable**

I am **grateful** for...

✦ _____

✦ _____

✦ _____

Part II: To be filled out at night

Two **happy moments** I had today were...

✦ _____

✦ _____

_____

One **accomplishment** I had today was...

✦ _____

My **Happiness Trophy** goes to:

✦ _____

An **act of kindness** I did today was...

✦ _____

_____

A **conscious struggle** I have is...

✦ _____

_____

_____

Overall my day was...

☺ ☺ ☹

Part I: To be filled out in the morning   Date: _____ / _____ / _____

My **happiness-source goals** for today are...

Something **meaningful**	Something **pleasurable**
Something **challenging**	Something **unpleasurable**

I am **grateful** for...

⬩ _____

⬩ _____

⬩ _____

Part II: To be filled out at night

Two **happy moments** I had today were...

⬩ _____

⬩ _____

_____

One **accomplishment** I had today was...

⬩ _____

My **Happiness Trophy** goes to:

⬩ _____

An **act of kindness** I did today was...

⬩ _____

_____

A **conscious struggle** I have is...

⬩ _____

_____

_____

Overall my day was...

☺ 😐 ☹

108

Part I: To be filled out in the morning   Date: ____ / ____ / ____

My **happiness-source goals** for today are…

Something **meaningful**	Something **pleasurable**
Something **challenging**	Something **unpleasurable**

I am **grateful** for…

+ _____
+ _____
+ _____

Part II: To be filled out at night

Two **happy moments** I had today were…

+ _____
+ _____

An **act of kindness** I did today was…

+ _____
_____

One **accomplishment** I had today was…

+ _____

A **conscious struggle** I have is…

+ _____
_____

My **Happiness Trophy** goes to:

+ _____

Overall my day was…

☺ 😐 ☹

Part I: To be filled out in the morning   Date: _____ / _____ / _____

My **happiness-source goals** for today are...

Something **meaningful**	Something **pleasurable**
Something **challenging**	Something **unpleasurable**

I am **grateful** for...

+ _____

+ _____

+ _____

Part II: To be filled out at night

Two **happy moments** I had today were...

+ _____

+ _____

An **act of kindness** I did today was...

+ _____

_____

One **accomplishment** I had today was...

+ _____

A **conscious struggle** I have is...

+ _____

_____

_____

My **Happiness Trophy** goes to:

+ _____

Overall my day was...

☺ ☺ ☹

Part I: To be filled out in the morning   Date: _____ / _____ / _____

My **happiness-source goals** for today are…

Something **meaningful**	Something **pleasurable**
Something **challenging**	Something **unpleasurable**

I am **grateful** for…

⚜ _____

⚜ _____

⚜ _____

Part II: To be filled out at night

Two **happy moments** I had today were…

⚜ _____

⚜ _____

_____

One **accomplishment** I had today was…

⚜ _____

My **Happiness Trophy** goes to:

⚜ _____

An **act of kindness** I did today was…

⚜ _____

_____

A **conscious struggle** I have is…

⚜ _____

_____

_____

Overall my day was…

☺ 😐 ☹

Part I: To be filled out in the morning   Date: ____ / ____ / ____

My **happiness-source goals** for today are...

Something **meaningful**	Something **pleasurable**
Something **challenging**	Something **unpleasurable**

I am **grateful** for...

🌾 _____

🌾 _____

🌾 _____

Part II: To be filled out at night

Two **happy moments** I had today were...

🌾 _____

🌾 _____
_____

An **act of kindness** I did today was...

🌾 _____
_____

One **accomplishment** I had today was...

🌾 _____

A **conscious struggle** I have is...

🌾 _____
_____
_____

My **Happiness Trophy** goes to:

🌾 _____

Overall my day was...

☺ 😐 ☹

Part I: To be filled out in the morning   Date: ____ / ____ / ____

My **happiness-source goals** for today are…

Something **meaningful**	Something **pleasurable**
Something **challenging**	Something **unpleasurable**

I am **grateful** for…

⚜ _____

⚜ _____

⚜ _____

Part II: To be filled out at night

Two **happy moments** I had today were…

⚜ _____

⚜ _____

_____

An **act of kindness** I did today was…

⚜ _____

_____

One **accomplishment** I had today was…

⚜ _____

A **conscious struggle** I have is…

⚜ _____

_____

_____

My **Happiness Trophy** goes to:

⚜ _____

Overall my day was...

☺ 😐 ☹

Part I: To be filled out in the morning   Date: ____ / ____ / ____

My **happiness-source goals** for today are...

Something **meaningful**	Something **pleasurable**
Something **challenging**	Something **unpleasurable**

I am **grateful** for...

⁕ _____

⁕ _____

⁕ _____

Part II: To be filled out at night

Two **happy moments** I had today were...

⁕ _____

⁕ _____

_____

An **act of kindness** I did today was...

⁕ _____

_____

One **accomplishment** I had today was...

⁕ _____

A **conscious struggle** I have is...

⁕ _____

_____

_____

My **Happiness Trophy** goes to:

⁕ _____

Overall my day was...

☺ ☹ ☹

Part I: To be filled out in the morning   Date: ____ / ____ / ____

My **happiness-source goals** for today are…

Something **meaningful**	Something **pleasurable**
Something **challenging**	Something **unpleasurable**

I am **grateful** for…

+ _____
+ _____
+ _____

Part II: To be filled out at night

Two **happy moments** I had today were…

+ _____
  _____
+ _____
  _____

An **act of kindness** I did today was…

+ _____
  _____

One **accomplishment** I had today was…

+ _____

A **conscious struggle** I have is…

+ _____
  _____
  _____

My **Happiness Trophy** goes to:

+ _____

Overall my day was…

☺ ☺ ☹

Part I: To be filled out in the morning   Date: ____ / ____ / ____

My **happiness-source goals** for today are...

Something **meaningful**	Something **pleasurable**
Something **challenging**	Something **unpleasurable**

I am **grateful** for...

+ _____

+ _____

+ _____

Part II: To be filled out at night

Two **happy moments** I had today were...

+ _____

+ _____

An **act of kindness** I did today was...

+ _____

One **accomplishment** I had today was...

+ _____

A **conscious struggle** I have is...

+ _____

My **Happiness Trophy** goes to:

+ _____

Overall my day was...

☺ 😐 ☹

Part I: To be filled out in the morning   Date: ____ / ____ / ____

My **happiness-source goals** for today are...

Something **meaningful**	Something **pleasurable**
Something **challenging**	Something **unpleasurable**

I am **grateful** for...

+ _____

+ _____

+ _____

Part II: To be filled out at night

Two **happy moments** I had today were...

+ _____

+ _____

_____

An **act of kindness** I did today was...

+ _____

_____

One **accomplishment** I had today was...

+ _____

A **conscious struggle** I have is...

+ _____

_____

_____

My **Happiness Trophy** goes to:

+ _____

Overall my day was...

☺ 😐 ☹

Part I: To be filled out in the morning   Date: ____ / ____ / ____

My **happiness-source goals** for today are…

Something **meaningful**	Something **pleasurable**
Something **challenging**	Something **unpleasurable**

I am **grateful** for…

⊥ _____

⊥ _____

⊥ _____

Part II: To be filled out at night

Two **happy moments** I had today were…

⊥ _____

⊥ _____
_____

An **act of kindness** I did today was…

⊥ _____
_____

One **accomplishment** I had today was…

⊥ _____

A **conscious struggle** I have is…

⊥ _____
_____
_____

My **Happiness Trophy** goes to:

⊥ _____

Overall my day was…

☺ ☺ ☹

Part I: To be filled out in the morning   Date: ____ / ____ / ____

My **happiness-source goals** for today are…

Something **meaningful**	Something **pleasurable**
Something **challenging**	Something **unpleasurable**

I am **grateful** for…

✦ _____

✦ _____

✦ _____

Part II: To be filled out at night

Two **happy moments** I had today were…

✦ _____

✦ _____

_____

An **act of kindness** I did today was…

✦ _____

_____

One **accomplishment** I had today was…

✦ _____

A **conscious struggle** I have is…

✦ _____

_____

_____

My **Happiness Trophy** goes to:

✦ _____

Overall my day was…

☺ 😐 ☹

Part I: To be filled out in the morning   Date: ____ / ____ / ____

My **happiness-source goals** for today are...

Something **meaningful**	Something **pleasurable**
Something **challenging**	Something **unpleasurable**

I am **grateful** for...

🕀 _____

🕀 _____

🕀 _____

Part II: To be filled out at night

Two **happy moments** I had today were...

🕀 _____

🕀 _____
_____

One **accomplishment** I had today was...

🕀 _____

My **Happiness Trophy** goes to:

🕀 _____

An **act of kindness** I did today was...

🕀 _____
_____

A **conscious struggle** I have is...

🕀 _____
_____
_____

Overall my day was...

☺ 😐 ☹

Part I: To be filled out in the morning   Date: ____ / ____ / ____

My **happiness-source goals** for today are…

Something **meaningful**	Something **pleasurable**
Something **challenging**	Something **unpleasurable**

I am **grateful** for…

* _____
* _____
* _____

Part II: To be filled out at night

Two **happy moments** I had today were…

* _____
* _____
  _____

An **act of kindness** I did today was…

* _____
  _____

One **accomplishment** I had today was…

* _____

A **conscious struggle** I have is…

* _____
  _____
  _____

My **Happiness Trophy** goes to:

* _____

Overall my day was…

☺ ☺ ☹

Part I: To be filled out in the morning   Date: ____ / ____ / ____

My **happiness-source goals** for today are…

Something **meaningful**	Something **pleasurable**
Something **challenging**	Something **unpleasurable**

I am **grateful** for…

+ _____

+ _____

+ _____

Part II: To be filled out at night

Two **happy moments** I had today were…

+ _____

+ _____

_____

An **act of kindness** I did today was…

+ _____

_____

One **accomplishment** I had today was…

+ _____

A **conscious struggle** I have is…

+ _____

_____

_____

My **Happiness Trophy** goes to:

+ _____

Overall my day was…

☺ ☺ ☹

Part I: To be filled out in the morning   Date: ____ / ____ / ____

My **happiness-source goals** for today are…

Something **meaningful**	Something **pleasurable**
Something **challenging**	Something **unpleasurable**

I am **grateful** for…

✦ _____

✦ _____

✦ _____

Part II: To be filled out at night

Two **happy moments** I had today were…

✦ _____

✦ _____

_____

An **act of kindness** I did today was…

✦ _____

_____

One **accomplishment** I had today was…

✦ _____

A **conscious struggle** I have is…

✦ _____

_____

_____

My **Happiness Trophy** goes to:

✦ _____

Overall my day was…

☺ 😐 ☹

Part I: To be filled out in the morning   Date: ___ / ___ / ___

My **happiness-source goals** for today are...

Something **meaningful**	Something **pleasurable**
Something **challenging**	Something **unpleasurable**

I am **grateful** for...

+ _____

+ _____

+ _____

Part II: To be filled out at night

Two **happy moments** I had today were...

+ _____

+ _____

_____

An **act of kindness** I did today was...

+ _____

_____

One **accomplishment** I had today was...

+ _____

A **conscious struggle** I have is...

+ _____

_____

_____

My **Happiness Trophy** goes to:

+ _____

Overall my day was...

☺ ☺ ☹

Part I: To be filled out in the morning   Date: ___ / ___ / ___

My **happiness-source goals** for today are…

Something **meaningful**	Something **pleasurable**
Something **challenging**	Something **unpleasurable**

I am **grateful** for…

_____

_____

_____

Part II: To be filled out at night

Two **happy moments** I had today were…

_____

_____

_____

One **accomplishment** I had today was…

_____

My **Happiness Trophy** goes to:

_____

An **act of kindness** I did today was…

_____

_____

A **conscious struggle** I have is…

_____

_____

_____

Overall my day was…

☺ ☺ ☹

Part I: To be filled out in the morning   Date: ____ / ____ / ____

My **happiness-source goals** for today are...

Something **meaningful**	Something **pleasurable**
Something **challenging**	Something **unpleasurable**

I am **grateful** for...

✦ _____

✦ _____

✦ _____

Part II: To be filled out at night

Two **happy moments** I had today were...

✦ _____

✦ _____

An **act of kindness** I did today was...

✦ _____

_____

One **accomplishment** I had today was...

✦ _____

A **conscious struggle** I have is...

✦ _____

_____

My **Happiness Trophy** goes to:

✦ _____

Overall my day was...

☺ 😐 ☹

Part I: To be filled out in the morning   Date: _____ / _____ / _____

My **happiness-source goals** for today are...

Something **meaningful**	Something **pleasurable**
Something **challenging**	Something **unpleasurable**

I am **grateful** for...

✦ _____

✦ _____

✦ _____

Part II: To be filled out at night

Two **happy moments** I had today were...

✦ _____

✦ _____

An **act of kindness** I did today was...

✦ _____

A **conscious struggle** I have is...

✦ _____

One **accomplishment** I had today was...

✦ _____

My **Happiness Trophy** goes to:

✦ _____

Overall my day was...

☺ 😐 ☹

Part I: To be filled out in the morning   Date: ____ / ____ / ____

My **happiness-source goals** for today are…

Something **meaningful**	Something **pleasurable**
Something **challenging**	Something **unpleasurable**

I am **grateful** for…

- _____
- _____
- _____

Part II: To be filled out at night

Two **happy moments** I had today were…
- _____
- _____
- _____

An **act of kindness** I did today was…
- _____
_____

One **accomplishment** I had today was…
- _____

A **conscious struggle** I have is…
- _____
_____
_____

My **Happiness Trophy** goes to:
- _____

Overall my day was…

☺ ☺ ☹

Part I: To be filled out in the morning   Date: _____ / _____ / _____

My **happiness-source goals** for today are…

Something **meaningful**	Something **pleasurable**
Something **challenging**	Something **unpleasurable**

I am **grateful** for…

➧ _____

➧ _____

➧ _____

Part II: To be filled out at night

Two **happy moments** I had today were…

➧ _____

➧ _____
_____

An **act of kindness** I did today was…

➧ _____
_____

One **accomplishment** I had today was…

➧ _____

A **conscious struggle** I have is…

➧ _____
_____
_____

My **Happiness Trophy** goes to:

➧ _____

Overall my day was…

☺ ☻ ☹

Part I: To be filled out in the morning   Date: ____ / ____ / ____

My **happiness-source goals** for today are…

Something **meaningful**	Something **pleasurable**
Something **challenging**	Something **unpleasurable**

I am **grateful** for…

🜲 _____

🜲 _____

🜲 _____

Part II: To be filled out at night

Two **happy moments** I had today were…

🜲 _____

🜲 _____

_____

One **accomplishment** I had today was…

🜲 _____

My **Happiness Trophy** goes to:

🜲 _____

An **act of kindness** I did today was…

🜲 _____

_____

A **conscious struggle** I have is…

🜲 _____

_____

_____

Overall my day was…

☺ ☺ ☹

Part I: To be filled out in the morning   Date: ____ / ____ / ____

My **happiness-source goals** for today are…

Something **meaningful**	Something **pleasurable**
Something **challenging**	Something **unpleasurable**

I am **grateful** for…

+ _____
+ _____
+ _____

Part II: To be filled out at night

Two **happy moments** I had today were…

+ _____
+ _____

An **act of kindness** I did today was…

+ _____
  _____

One **accomplishment** I had today was…

+ _____

A **conscious struggle** I have is…

+ _____
  _____
  _____

My **Happiness Trophy** goes to:

+ _____

Overall my day was…

☺ 😐 ☹

Part I: To be filled out in the morning   Date: ____ / ____ / ____

My **happiness-source goals** for today are...

Something **meaningful**	Something **pleasurable**
Something **challenging**	Something **unpleasurable**

I am **grateful** for...

🔸 _____

🔸 _____

🔸 _____

Part II: To be filled out at night

Two **happy moments** I had today were...

🔸 _____

🔸 _____

_____

An **act of kindness** I did today was...

🔸 _____

_____

One **accomplishment** I had today was...

🔸 _____

A **conscious struggle** I have is...

🔸 _____

_____

_____

My **Happiness Trophy** goes to:

🔸 _____

Overall my day was...

☺ 😐 ☹

Part I: To be filled out in the morning   Date: ____ / ____ / ____

My **happiness-source goals** for today are...

Something **meaningful**	Something **pleasurable**
Something **challenging**	Something **unpleasurable**

I am **grateful** for...

+ _____

+ _____

+ _____

Part II: To be filled out at night

Two **happy moments** I had today were...

+ _____

+ _____

_____

An **act of kindness** I did today was...

+ _____

_____

One **accomplishment** I had today was...

+ _____

A **conscious struggle** I have is...

+ _____

_____

_____

My **Happiness Trophy** goes to:

+ _____

Overall my day was...

☺ ☻ ☹

Part I: To be filled out in the morning   Date: ____ / ____ / ____

My **happiness-source goals** for today are...

Something **meaningful**	Something **pleasurable**
Something **challenging**	Something **unpleasurable**

I am **grateful** for...

+ _____

+ _____

+ _____

Part II: To be filled out at night

Two **happy moments** I had today were...

+ _____

+ _____

_____

An **act of kindness** I did today was...

+ _____

_____

One **accomplishment** I had today was...

+ _____

A **conscious struggle** I have is...

+ _____

_____

_____

My **Happiness Trophy** goes to:

+ _____

Overall my day was...

☺ ☺ ☹

Part I: To be filled out in the morning   Date: ____ / ____ / ____

My **happiness-source goals** for today are…

Something **meaningful**	Something **pleasurable**
Something **challenging**	Something **unpleasurable**

I am **grateful** for…

🕂 _____

🕂 _____

🕂 _____

Part II: To be filled out at night

Two **happy moments** I had today were…

🕂 _____

🕂 _____

_____

An **act of kindness** I did today was…

🕂 _____

_____

One **accomplishment** I had today was…

🕂 _____

A **conscious struggle** I have is…

🕂 _____

_____

_____

My **Happiness Trophy** goes to:

🕂 _____

Overall my day was…

🙂 😐 ☹️

Part I: To be filled out in the morning   Date: ____ / ____ / ____

My **happiness-source goals** for today are...

Something **meaningful**	Something **pleasurable**
Something **challenging**	Something **unpleasurable**

I am **grateful** for...

- _____
- _____
- _____

Part II: To be filled out at night

Two **happy moments** I had today were...
- _____
- _____

An **act of kindness** I did today was...
- _____
  _____

One **accomplishment** I had today was...
- _____

A **conscious struggle** I have is...
- _____
  _____
  _____

My **Happiness Trophy** goes to:
- _____

Overall my day was...

☺ ☺ ☹

Part I: To be filled out in the morning   Date: ____ / ____ / ____

My **happiness-source goals** for today are…

Something **meaningful**	Something **pleasurable**
Something **challenging**	Something **unpleasurable**

I am **grateful** for…

- _____
- _____
- _____

Part II: To be filled out at night

Two **happy moments** I had today were…

- _____
- _____

One **accomplishment** I had today was…

- _____

My **Happiness Trophy** goes to:

- _____

An **act of kindness** I did today was…

- _____
- _____

A **conscious struggle** I have is…

- _____
- _____

Overall my day was...

☺ ☺ ☹

Part I: To be filled out in the morning   Date: _____ / _____ / _____

My **happiness-source goals** for today are...

Something **meaningful**	Something **pleasurable**
Something **challenging**	Something **unpleasurable**

I am **grateful** for...

🔸 _____

🔸 _____

🔸 _____

Part II: To be filled out at night

Two **happy moments** I had today were...

🔸 _____

🔸 _____

_____

An **act of kindness** I did today was...

🔸 _____

_____

One **accomplishment** I had today was...

🔸 _____

A **conscious struggle** I have is...

🔸 _____

_____

_____

My **Happiness Trophy** goes to:

🔸 _____

Overall my day was...

☺ 😐 ☹

Part I: To be filled out in the morning   Date: _____ / _____ / _____

My **happiness-source goals** for today are...

Something **meaningful**	Something **pleasurable**
Something **challenging**	Something **unpleasurable**

I am **grateful** for...

+ _____

+ _____

+ _____

Part II: To be filled out at night

Two **happy moments** I had today were...

+ _____

+ _____

An **act of kindness** I did today was...

+ _____

One **accomplishment** I had today was...

+ _____

A **conscious struggle** I have is...

+ _____

My **Happiness Trophy** goes to:

+ _____

Overall my day was...

☺ 😐 ☹

Part I: To be filled out in the morning   Date: ___ / ___ / ___

My **happiness-source goals** for today are…

Something **meaningful**	Something **pleasurable**
Something **challenging**	Something **unpleasurable**

I am **grateful** for…

🔸 _____

🔸 _____

🔸 _____

Part II: To be filled out at night

Two **happy moments** I had today were…

🔸 _____

🔸 _____

_____

An **act of kindness** I did today was…

🔸 _____

_____

One **accomplishment** I had today was…

🔸 _____

A **conscious struggle** I have is…

🔸 _____

_____

_____

My **Happiness Trophy** goes to:

🔸 _____

Overall my day was…

☺ 😐 ☹

Part I: To be filled out in the morning   Date: ____ / ____ / ____

My **happiness-source goals** for today are…

Something **meaningful**	Something **pleasurable**
Something **challenging**	Something **unpleasurable**

I am **grateful** for…

⁜ _____

⁜ _____

⁜ _____

Part II: To be filled out at night

Two **happy moments** I had today were…

⁜ _____

⁜ _____

One **accomplishment** I had today was…

⁜ _____

My **Happiness Trophy** goes to:

⁜ _____

An **act of kindness** I did today was…

⁜ _____

A **conscious struggle** I have is…

⁜ _____

Overall my day was…

☺ ☹ ☹

Part I: To be filled out in the morning   Date: ____ / ____ / ____

My **happiness-source goals** for today are…

Something **meaningful**	Something **pleasurable**
Something **challenging**	Something **unpleasurable**

I am **grateful** for…

- _____
- _____
- _____

Part II: To be filled out at night

Two **happy moments** I had today were…
- _____
- _____

An **act of kindness** I did today was…
- _____

One **accomplishment** I had today was…
- _____

A **conscious struggle** I have is…
- _____

My **Happiness Trophy** goes to:
- _____

Overall my day was…

☺ 😐 ☹

Part I: To be filled out in the morning   Date: ___ / ___ / ___

My **happiness-source goals** for today are…

Something **meaningful**	Something **pleasurable**
Something **challenging**	Something **unpleasurable**

I am **grateful** for…

- _____
- _____
- _____

Part II: To be filled out at night

Two **happy moments** I had today were…
- _____
- _____
_____

An **act of kindness** I did today was…
- _____
_____

One **accomplishment** I had today was…
- _____

A **conscious struggle** I have is…
- _____
_____
_____

My **Happiness Trophy** goes to:
- _____

Overall my day was…

☺ ☺ ☹

Part I: To be filled out in the morning   Date: ____ / ____ / ____

My **happiness-source goals** for today are...

Something **meaningful**	Something **pleasurable**
Something **challenging**	Something **unpleasurable**

I am **grateful** for...

- _____
- _____
- _____

Part II: To be filled out at night

Two **happy moments** I had today were...
- _____
- _____

An **act of kindness** I did today was...
- _____
- _____

One **accomplishment** I had today was...
- _____

A **conscious struggle** I have is...
- _____
- _____

My **Happiness Trophy** goes to:
- _____

Overall my day was...

☺ ☻ ☹

Part I: To be filled out in the morning   Date: ＿＿ / ＿＿ / ＿＿

My **happiness-source goals** for today are…

Something **meaningful**	Something **pleasurable**
Something **challenging**	Something **unpleasurable**

I am **grateful** for…

✦ _____

✦ _____

✦ _____

Part II: To be filled out at night

Two **happy moments** I had today were…

✦ _____

✦ _____

An **act of kindness** I did today was…

✦ _____

One **accomplishment** I had today was…

✦ _____

A **conscious struggle** I have is…

✦ _____

My **Happiness Trophy** goes to:

✦ _____

Overall my day was…

☺ ☻ ☹

Part I: To be filled out in the morning   Date: ___ / ___ / ___

My **happiness-source goals** for today are…

Something **meaningful**	Something **pleasurable**
Something **challenging**	Something **unpleasurable**

I am **grateful** for…

+ _____

+ _____

+ _____

Part II: To be filled out at night

Two **happy moments** I had today were…

+ _____

+ _____

_____

An **act of kindness** I did today was…

+ _____

_____

One **accomplishment** I had today was…

+ _____

A **conscious struggle** I have is…

+ _____

_____

_____

My **Happiness Trophy** goes to:

+ _____

Overall my day was…

☺ ☹ ☹

Part I: To be filled out in the morning   Date: ____ / ____ / ____

My **happiness-source goals** for today are…

Something **meaningful**	Something **pleasurable**
Something **challenging**	Something **unpleasurable**

I am **grateful** for…

♣ _____

♣ _____

♣ _____

Part II: To be filled out at night

Two **happy moments** I had today were…

♣ _____

♣ _____

An **act of kindness** I did today was…

♣ _____

One **accomplishment** I had today was…

♣ _____

A **conscious struggle** I have is…

♣ _____

My **Happiness Trophy** goes to:

♣ _____

Overall my day was…

☺ ☹ ☹

Part I: To be filled out in the morning   Date: ____ / ____ / ____

My **happiness-source goals** for today are...

Something **meaningful**	Something **pleasurable**
Something **challenging**	Something **unpleasurable**

I am **grateful** for...

+ _____

+ _____

+ _____

Part II: To be filled out at night

Two **happy moments** I had today were...

+ _____

+ _____

_____

An **act of kindness** I did today was...

+ _____

_____

One **accomplishment** I had today was...

+ _____

A **conscious struggle** I have is...

+ _____

_____

_____

My **Happiness Trophy** goes to:

+ _____

Overall my day was...

☺ ☻ ☹

Part I: To be filled out in the morning   Date: ____ / ____ / ____

My **happiness-source goals** for today are…

Something **meaningful**	Something **pleasurable**
Something **challenging**	Something **unpleasurable**

I am **grateful** for…

🔸 _____

🔸 _____

🔸 _____

Part II: To be filled out at night

Two **happy moments** I had today were…

🔸 _____

🔸 _____

_____

An **act of kindness** I did today was…

🔸 _____

_____

One **accomplishment** I had today was…

🔸 _____

A **conscious struggle** I have is…

🔸 _____

_____

_____

My **Happiness Trophy** goes to:

🔸 _____

Overall my day was…

☺ 😐 ☹

Part I: To be filled out in the morning   Date: ____ / ____ / ____

My **happiness-source goals** for today are...

Something **meaningful**	Something **pleasurable**
Something **challenging**	Something **unpleasurable**

I am **grateful** for...

- _____
- _____
- _____

Part II: To be filled out at night

Two **happy moments** I had today were...
- _____
- _____

One **accomplishment** I had today was...
- _____

My **Happiness Trophy** goes to:
- _____

An **act of kindness** I did today was...
- _____
- _____

A **conscious struggle** I have is...
- _____
- _____
- _____

Overall my day was...

☺ ☹ ☹

Part I: To be filled out in the morning   Date: _____ / _____ / _____

My **happiness-source goals** for today are...

Something **meaningful**	Something **pleasurable**
Something **challenging**	Something **unpleasurable**

I am **grateful** for...

- _____
- _____
- _____

Part II: To be filled out at night

Two **happy moments** I had today were...
- _____
- _____
_____

One **accomplishment** I had today was...
- _____

My **Happiness Trophy** goes to:
- _____

An **act of kindness** I did today was...
- _____
_____

A **conscious struggle** I have is...
- _____
_____
_____

Overall my day was...

☺ ☺ ☹

Part I: To be filled out in the morning   Date: ____ / ____ /____

My **happiness-source goals** for today are…

Something **meaningful**	Something **pleasurable**
Something **challenging**	Something **unpleasurable**

I am **grateful** for…

🍀 _____

🍀 _____

🍀 _____

Part II: To be filled out at night

Two **happy moments** I had today were…

🍀 _____

🍀 _____

    _____

An **act of kindness** I did today was…

🍀 _____

    _____

One **accomplishment** I had today was…

🍀 _____

A **conscious struggle** I have is…

🍀 _____

    _____

    _____

My **Happiness Trophy** goes to:

🍀 _____

Overall my day was…

☺ 😐 ☹

Part I: To be filled out in the morning   Date: ____ / ____ / ____

My **happiness-source goals** for today are…

Something **meaningful**	Something **pleasurable**
Something **challenging**	Something **unpleasurable**

I am **grateful** for…

+ _____

+ _____

+ _____

Part II: To be filled out at night

Two **happy moments** I had today were…

+ _____

+ _____

_____

An **act of kindness** I did today was…

+ _____

_____

One **accomplishment** I had today was…

+ _____

A **conscious struggle** I have is…

+ _____

_____

_____

My **Happiness Trophy** goes to:

+ _____

Overall my day was…

☺ ☺ ☹

Part I: To be filled out in the morning   Date: ____ / ____ / ____

My **happiness-source goals** for today are…

Something **meaningful**	Something **pleasurable**
Something **challenging**	Something **unpleasurable**

I am **grateful** for…

🕂 _____

🕂 _____

🕂 _____

Part II: To be filled out at night

Two **happy moments** I had today were…

🕂 _____

🕂 _____

_____

An **act of kindness** I did today was…

🕂 _____

_____

One **accomplishment** I had today was…

🕂 _____

A **conscious struggle** I have is…

🕂 _____

_____

_____

My **Happiness Trophy** goes to:

🕂 _____

Overall my day was…

☺ 😐 ☹

Part I: To be filled out in the morning   Date: ____ / ____ / ____

My **happiness-source goals** for today are…

Something **meaningful**	Something **pleasurable**
Something **challenging**	Something **unpleasurable**

I am **grateful** for…

+ _____

+ _____

+ _____

Part II: To be filled out at night

Two **happy moments** I had today were…

+ _____

+ _____

_____

An **act of kindness** I did today was…

+ _____

_____

One **accomplishment** I had today was…

+ _____

A **conscious struggle** I have is…

+ _____

_____

_____

My **Happiness Trophy** goes to:

+ _____

Overall my day was…

☺ ☻ ☹

Part I: To be filled out in the morning   Date: ____ / ____ / ____

My **happiness-source goals** for today are...

Something **meaningful**	Something **pleasurable**
Something **challenging**	Something **unpleasurable**

I am **grateful** for...

🌿 _____

🌿 _____

🌿 _____

Part II: To be filled out at night

Two **happy moments** I had today were...

🌿 _____

🌿 _____

_____

One **accomplishment** I had today was...

🌿 _____

My **Happiness Trophy** goes to:

🌿 _____

An **act of kindness** I did today was...

🌿 _____

_____

A **conscious struggle** I have is...

🌿 _____

_____

_____

Overall my day was...

☺ 😐 ☹

Part I: To be filled out in the morning   Date: _____ / _____ / _____

My **happiness-source goals** for today are…

Something **meaningful**	Something **pleasurable**
Something **challenging**	Something **unpleasurable**

I am **grateful** for…

✦ _____

✦ _____

✦ _____

Part II: To be filled out at night

Two **happy moments** I had today were…

✦ _____

✦ _____

_____

An **act of kindness** I did today was…

✦ _____

_____

One **accomplishment** I had today was…

✦ _____

A **conscious struggle** I have is…

✦ _____

_____

_____

My **Happiness Trophy** goes to:

✦ _____

Overall my day was…

☺ 😐 ☹

Part I: To be filled out in the morning   Date: ____ / ____ / ____

My **happiness-source goals** for today are…

Something **meaningful**	Something **pleasurable**
Something **challenging**	Something **unpleasurable**

I am **grateful** for…

🌿 _____

🌿 _____

🌿 _____

Part II: To be filled out at night

Two **happy moments** I had today were…

🌿 _____

🌿 _____

_____

An **act of kindness** I did today was…

🌿 _____

_____

One **accomplishment** I had today was…

🌿 _____

A **conscious struggle** I have is…

🌿 _____

_____

_____

My **Happiness Trophy** goes to:

🌿 _____

Overall my day was…

☺ 😐 ☹

Part I: To be filled out in the morning   Date: _____ / _____ / _____

My **happiness-source goals** for today are...

Something **meaningful**	Something **pleasurable**
Something **challenging**	Something **unpleasurable**

I am **grateful** for...

⚜ _____

⚜ _____

⚜ _____

Part II: To be filled out at night

Two **happy moments** I had today were...

⚜ _____

⚜ _____

_____

An **act of kindness** I did today was...

⚜ _____

_____

One **accomplishment** I had today was...

⚜ _____

A **conscious struggle** I have is...

⚜ _____

_____

_____

My **Happiness Trophy** goes to:

⚜ _____

Overall my day was...

☺ 😐 ☹

Part I: To be filled out in the morning   Date: _____ / _____ / _____

My **happiness-source goals** for today are...

Something **meaningful**	Something **pleasurable**
Something **challenging**	Something **unpleasurable**

I am **grateful** for...

🌿 _____

🌿 _____

🌿 _____

Part II: To be filled out at night

Two **happy moments** I had today were...

🌿 _____

🌿 _____

_____

An **act of kindness** I did today was...

🌿 _____

_____

One **accomplishment** I had today was...

🌿 _____

A **conscious struggle** I have is...

🌿 _____

_____

_____

My **Happiness Trophy** goes to:

🌿 _____

Overall my day was...

☺ 😐 ☹

Part I: To be filled out in the morning   Date: ____ / ____ / ____

My **happiness-source goals** for today are...

Something **meaningful**	Something **pleasurable**
Something **challenging**	Something **unpleasurable**

I am **grateful** for...

⁕ _____

⁕ _____

⁕ _____

Part II: To be filled out at night

Two **happy moments** I had today were...

⁕ _____

⁕ _____

_____

An **act of kindness** I did today was...

⁕ _____

_____

One **accomplishment** I had today was...

⁕ _____

A **conscious struggle** I have is...

⁕ _____

_____

_____

My **Happiness Trophy** goes to:

⁕ _____

Overall my day was...

☺ 😐 ☹

Part I: To be filled out in the morning   Date: _____ / _____ / _____

My **happiness-source goals** for today are…

Something **meaningful**	Something **pleasurable**
Something **challenging**	Something **unpleasurable**

I am **grateful** for…

+ _____

+ _____

+ _____

Part II: To be filled out at night

Two **happy moments** I had today were…

+ _____

+ _____

_____

An **act of kindness** I did today was…

+ _____

_____

One **accomplishment** I had today was…

+ _____

A **conscious struggle** I have is…

+ _____

_____

_____

My **Happiness Trophy** goes to:

+ _____

Overall my day was…

☺ ☺ ☹

Part I: To be filled out in the morning   Date: ____ / ____ / ____

My **happiness-source goals** for today are...

Something **meaningful**	Something **pleasurable**
Something **challenging**	Something **unpleasurable**

I am **grateful** for...

+ _____

+ _____

+ _____

Part II: To be filled out at night

Two **happy moments** I had today were...

+ _____

+ _____

An **act of kindness** I did today was...

+ _____
_____

One **accomplishment** I had today was...

+ _____

A **conscious struggle** I have is...

+ _____
_____
_____

My **Happiness Trophy** goes to:

+ _____

Overall my day was...

☺ ☺ ☹

Part I: To be filled out in the morning   Date: ____ / ____ / ____

My **happiness-source goals** for today are…

Something **meaningful**	Something **pleasurable**
Something **challenging**	Something **unpleasurable**

I am **grateful** for…

+ _____

+ _____

+ _____

Part II: To be filled out at night

Two **happy moments** I had today were…

+ _____

+ _____

_____

An **act of kindness** I did today was…

+ _____

_____

One **accomplishment** I had today was…

+ _____

A **conscious struggle** I have is…

+ _____

_____

_____

My **Happiness Trophy** goes to:

+ _____

Overall my day was…

☺ ☺ ☹

Part I: To be filled out in the morning   Date: ____ / ____ / ____

My **happiness-source goals** for today are…

Something **meaningful**	Something **pleasurable**
Something **challenging**	Something **unpleasurable**

I am **grateful** for…

⚜ _____

⚜ _____

⚜ _____

Part II: To be filled out at night

Two **happy moments** I had today were…

⚜ _____

⚜ _____

_____

An **act of kindness** I did today was…

⚜ _____

_____

A **conscious struggle** I have is…

⚜ _____

_____

_____

One **accomplishment** I had today was…

⚜ _____

My **Happiness Trophy** goes to:

⚜ _____

Overall my day was…

☺ 😐 ☹

Part I: To be filled out in the morning   Date: ____ / ____ / ____

My **happiness-source goals** for today are…

Something **meaningful**	Something **pleasurable**
Something **challenging**	Something **unpleasurable**

I am **grateful** for…

+ _____

+ _____

+ _____

Part II: To be filled out at night

Two **happy moments** I had today were…

+ _____

+ _____

  _____

One **accomplishment** I had today was…

+ _____

My **Happiness Trophy** goes to:

+ _____

An **act of kindness** I did today was…

+ _____

  _____

A **conscious struggle** I have is…

+ _____

  _____

  _____

Overall my day was…

☺ ☻ ☹

Part I: To be filled out in the morning   Date: ____ / ____ / ____

My **happiness-source goals** for today are...

Something **meaningful**	Something **pleasurable**
Something **challenging**	Something **unpleasurable**

I am **grateful** for...

✦ _____

✦ _____

✦ _____

Part II: To be filled out at night

Two **happy moments** I had today were...

✦ _____

✦ _____

_____

An **act of kindness** I did today was...

✦ _____

_____

One **accomplishment** I had today was...

✦ _____

A **conscious struggle** I have is...

✦ _____

_____

_____

My **Happiness Trophy** goes to:

✦ _____

Overall my day was...

☺ ☺ ☹

Part I: To be filled out in the morning   Date: ____ / ____ / ____

My **happiness-source goals** for today are...

Something **meaningful**	Something **pleasurable**
Something **challenging**	Something **unpleasurable**

I am **grateful** for...

✦ _____

✦ _____

✦ _____

Part II: To be filled out at night

Two **happy moments** I had today were...

✦ _____

✦ _____
_____

One **accomplishment** I had today was...

✦ _____

My **Happiness Trophy** goes to:

✦ _____

An **act of kindness** I did today was...

✦ _____
_____

A **conscious struggle** I have is...

✦ _____
_____
_____

Overall my day was...

☺ ☺ ☹

Part I: To be filled out in the morning   Date: ____ / ____ / ____

My **happiness-source goals** for today are…

Something **meaningful**	Something **pleasurable**
Something **challenging**	Something **unpleasurable**

I am **grateful** for…

+ _____

+ _____

+ _____

Part II: To be filled out at night

Two **happy moments** I had today were…

+ _____

+ _____

An **act of kindness** I did today was…

+ _____

One **accomplishment** I had today was…

+ _____

A **conscious struggle** I have is…

+ _____

My **Happiness Trophy** goes to:

+ _____

Overall my day was…

☺ ☺ ☹

Part I: To be filled out in the morning   Date: _____ / _____ / _____

My **happiness-source goals** for today are…

Something **meaningful**	Something **pleasurable**
Something **challenging**	Something **unpleasurable**

I am **grateful** for…

🔸 _____

🔸 _____

🔸 _____

Part II: To be filled out at night

Two **happy moments** I had today were…

🔸 _____

🔸 _____

_____

An **act of kindness** I did today was…

🔸 _____

_____

One **accomplishment** I had today was…

🔸 _____

A **conscious struggle** I have is…

🔸 _____

_____

_____

My **Happiness Trophy** goes to:

🔸 _____

Overall my day was…

☺ 😐 ☹

Part I: To be filled out in the morning   Date: ____ / ____ / ____

My **happiness-source goals** for today are…

Something **meaningful**	Something **pleasurable**
Something **challenging**	Something **unpleasurable**

I am **grateful** for…

- _____
- _____
- _____

Part II: To be filled out at night

Two **happy moments** I had today were…

- _____
- _____

An **act of kindness** I did today was…

- _____

One **accomplishment** I had today was…

- _____

A **conscious struggle** I have is…

- _____

My **Happiness Trophy** goes to:

- _____

Overall my day was…

☺ ☺ ☹

Part I: To be filled out in the morning   Date: ____ / ____ / ____

My **happiness-source goals** for today are...

Something **meaningful**	Something **pleasurable**
Something **challenging**	Something **unpleasurable**

I am **grateful** for...

+ _____

+ _____

+ _____

Part II: To be filled out at night

Two **happy moments** I had today were...

+ _____

+ _____

  _____

An **act of kindness** I did today was...

+ _____

  _____

One **accomplishment** I had today was...

+ _____

A **conscious struggle** I have is...

+ _____

  _____

  _____

My **Happiness Trophy** goes to:

+ _____

Overall my day was...

☺ ☺ ☹

Part I: To be filled out in the morning   Date: ____ / ____ / ____

My **happiness-source goals** for today are...

Something **meaningful**	Something **pleasurable**
Something **challenging**	Something **unpleasurable**

I am **grateful** for...

+ _____

+ _____

+ _____

Part II: To be filled out at night

Two **happy moments** I had today were...

+ _____

+ _____

One **accomplishment** I had today was...

+ _____

My **Happiness Trophy** goes to:

+ _____

An **act of kindness** I did today was...

+ _____

A **conscious struggle** I have is...

+ _____

Overall my day was...

☺ 😐 ☹

Part I: To be filled out in the morning   Date: ____ / ____ / ____

My **happiness-source goals** for today are...

Something **meaningful**	Something **pleasurable**
Something **challenging**	Something **unpleasurable**

I am **grateful** for...

+ _____

+ _____

+ _____

Part II: To be filled out at night

Two **happy moments** I had today were...

+ _____

+ _____
   _____

One **accomplishment** I had today was...

+ _____

My **Happiness Trophy** goes to:

+ _____

An **act of kindness** I did today was...

+ _____
   _____

A **conscious struggle** I have is...

+ _____
   _____
   _____

Overall my day was...

☺ ☻ ☹

Part I: To be filled out in the morning   Date: ____ / ____ / ____

My **happiness-source goals** for today are...

Something **meaningful**	Something **pleasurable**
Something **challenging**	Something **unpleasurable**

I am **grateful** for...

+ _____

+ _____

+ _____

Part II: To be filled out at night

Two **happy moments** I had today were...

+ _____

+ _____
  _____

An **act of kindness** I did today was...

+ _____
  _____

One **accomplishment** I had today was...

+ _____

A **conscious struggle** I have is...

+ _____
  _____
  _____

My **Happiness Trophy** goes to:

+ _____

Overall my day was...

☺ ☺ ☹

Part I: To be filled out in the morning   Date: _____ / _____ / _____

My **happiness-source goals** for today are…

Something **meaningful**	Something **pleasurable**
Something **challenging**	Something **unpleasurable**

I am **grateful** for…

🔸 _____

🔸 _____

🔸 _____

Part II: To be filled out at night

Two **happy moments** I had today were…

🔸 _____

🔸 _____
_____

An **act of kindness** I did today was…

🔸 _____
_____

One **accomplishment** I had today was…

🔸 _____

A **conscious struggle** I have is…

🔸 _____
_____
_____

My **Happiness Trophy** goes to:

🔸 _____

Overall my day was…

☺ 😐 ☹

Part I: To be filled out in the morning   Date: _____ / _____ / _____

My **happiness-source goals** for today are...

Something **meaningful**	Something **pleasurable**
Something **challenging**	Something **unpleasurable**

I am **grateful** for...

_____

_____

_____

Part II: To be filled out at night

Two **happy moments** I had today were...

_____

_____

_____

One **accomplishment** I had today was...

_____

My **Happiness Trophy** goes to:

_____

An **act of kindness** I did today was...

_____

_____

A **conscious struggle** I have is...

_____

_____

_____

Overall my day was...

☺ 😐 ☹

Part I: To be filled out in the morning   Date: _____ / _____ / _____

My **happiness-source goals** for today are…

Something **meaningful**	Something **pleasurable**
Something **challenging**	Something **unpleasurable**

I am **grateful** for…

⚜ _____

⚜ _____

⚜ _____

Part II: To be filled out at night

Two **happy moments** I had today were…

⚜ _____

⚜ _____

_____

An **act of kindness** I did today was…

⚜ _____

_____

One **accomplishment** I had today was…

⚜ _____

A **conscious struggle** I have is…

⚜ _____

_____

_____

My **Happiness Trophy** goes to:

⚜ _____

Overall my day was…

☺ 😐 ☹

Part I: To be filled out in the morning   Date: ____ / ____ / ____

My **happiness-source goals** for today are…

Something **meaningful**	Something **pleasurable**
Something **challenging**	Something **unpleasurable**

I am **grateful** for…

🞜 _____

🞜 _____

🞜 _____

Part II: To be filled out at night

Two **happy moments** I had today were…

🞜 _____

🞜 _____

_____

An **act of kindness** I did today was…

🞜 _____

_____

One **accomplishment** I had today was…

🞜 _____

A **conscious struggle** I have is…

🞜 _____

_____

_____

My **Happiness Trophy** goes to:

🞜 _____

Overall my day was…

☺ 😐 ☹

Part I: To be filled out in the morning   Date: _____ / _____ / _____

My **happiness-source goals** for today are...

Something **meaningful**	Something **pleasurable**
Something **challenging**	Something **unpleasurable**

I am **grateful** for...

↓ _____

↓ _____

↓ _____

Part II: To be filled out at night

Two **happy moments** I had today were...

↓ _____

↓ _____

_____

An **act of kindness** I did today was...

↓ _____

_____

One **accomplishment** I had today was...

↓ _____

A **conscious struggle** I have is...

↓ _____

_____

_____

My **Happiness Trophy** goes to:

↓ _____

Overall my day was...

☺ ☐ ☹

Part I: To be filled out in the morning   Date: _____ / _____ / _____

My **happiness-source goals** for today are...

Something **meaningful**	Something **pleasurable**
Something **challenging**	Something **unpleasurable**

I am **grateful** for...

* _____
* _____
* _____

Part II: To be filled out at night

Two **happy moments** I had today were...

* _____
* _____
  _____

An **act of kindness** I did today was...

* _____
  _____

One **accomplishment** I had today was...

* _____

A **conscious struggle** I have is...

* _____
  _____
  _____

My **Happiness Trophy** goes to:

* _____

Overall my day was...

☺ 😐 ☹

Part I: To be filled out in the morning   Date: ____ / ____ / ____

My **happiness-source goals** for today are…

Something **meaningful**	Something **pleasurable**
Something **challenging**	Something **unpleasurable**

I am **grateful** for…

- _____
- _____
- _____

Part II: To be filled out at night

Two **happy moments** I had today were…
- _____
- _____
  _____

An **act of kindness** I did today was…
- _____
  _____

One **accomplishment** I had today was…
- _____

A **conscious struggle** I have is…
- _____
  _____
  _____

My **Happiness Trophy** goes to:
- _____

Overall my day was…

☺ ☺ ☹

Part I: To be filled out in the morning   Date: ___ / ___ / ___

My **happiness-source goals** for today are…

Something **meaningful**	Something **pleasurable**
Something **challenging**	Something **unpleasurable**

I am **grateful** for…

+ _____

+ _____

+ _____

Part II: To be filled out at night

Two **happy moments** I had today were…

+ _____

+ _____

An **act of kindness** I did today was…

+ _____

_____

One **accomplishment** I had today was…

+ _____

A **conscious struggle** I have is…

+ _____

_____

_____

My **Happiness Trophy** goes to:

+ _____

Overall my day was…

☺ ☺ ☹

Part I: To be filled out in the morning   Date: ____ / ____ / ____

My **happiness-source goals** for today are...

Something **meaningful**	Something **pleasurable**
Something **challenging**	Something **unpleasurable**

I am **grateful** for...

+ _____

+ _____

+ _____

Part II: To be filled out at night

Two **happy moments** I had today were...

+ _____

+ _____

_____

One **accomplishment** I had today was...

+ _____

My **Happiness Trophy** goes to:

+ _____

An **act of kindness** I did today was...

+ _____

_____

A **conscious struggle** I have is...

+ _____

_____

_____

Overall my day was...

☺ ☺ ☹

Part I: To be filled out in the morning   Date: _____ / _____ / _____

My **happiness-source goals** for today are...

Something **meaningful**	Something **pleasurable**
Something **challenging**	Something **unpleasurable**

I am **grateful** for...

+ _____

+ _____

+ _____

Part II: To be filled out at night

Two **happy moments** I had today were...

+ _____

+ _____

_____

One **accomplishment** I had today was...

+ _____

My **Happiness Trophy** goes to:

+ _____

An **act of kindness** I did today was...

+ _____

_____

A **conscious struggle** I have is...

+ _____

_____

_____

Overall my day was...

☺ ☺ ☹

Part I: To be filled out in the morning   Date: _____ / _____ / _____

My **happiness-source goals** for today are...

Something **meaningful**	Something **pleasurable**
Something **challenging**	Something **unpleasurable**

I am **grateful** for...

+ _____
+ _____
+ _____

Part II: To be filled out at night

Two **happy moments** I had today were...

+ _____
+ _____
  _____

An **act of kindness** I did today was...

+ _____
  _____

One **accomplishment** I had today was...

+ _____

A **conscious struggle** I have is...

+ _____
  _____

My **Happiness Trophy** goes to:

+ _____

Overall my day was...

☺ ☺ ☹

Part I: To be filled out in the morning   Date: _____ / _____ / _____

My **happiness-source goals** for today are…

Something **meaningful**	Something **pleasurable**
Something **challenging**	Something **unpleasurable**

I am **grateful** for…

+ _____

+ _____

+ _____

Part II: To be filled out at night

Two **happy moments** I had today were…

+ _____

+ _____

_____

An **act of kindness** I did today was…

+ _____

_____

One **accomplishment** I had today was…

+ _____

A **conscious struggle** I have is…

+ _____

_____

_____

My **Happiness Trophy** goes to:

+ _____

Overall my day was…

☺ ☺ ☹

Part I: To be filled out in the morning   Date: ____ / ____ /____

My **happiness-source goals** for today are...

Something **meaningful**	Something **pleasurable**
Something **challenging**	Something **unpleasurable**

I am **grateful** for...

+ _____

+ _____

+ _____

Part II: To be filled out at night

Two **happy moments** I had today were...

+ _____

+ _____

_____

An **act of kindness** I did today was...

+ _____

_____

One **accomplishment** I had today was...

+ _____

A **conscious struggle** I have is...

+ _____

_____

_____

My **Happiness Trophy** goes to:

+ _____

Overall my day was...

☺ ☻ ☹

Part I: To be filled out in the morning   Date: _____ / _____ / _____

My **happiness-source goals** for today are...

Something **meaningful**	Something **pleasurable**
Something **challenging**	Something **unpleasurable**

I am **grateful** for...

+ _____

+ _____

+ _____

Part II: To be filled out at night

Two **happy moments** I had today were...

+ _____

+ _____
  _____

One **accomplishment** I had today was...

+ _____

My **Happiness Trophy** goes to:

+ _____

An **act of kindness** I did today was...

+ _____
  _____

A **conscious struggle** I have is...

+ _____
  _____
  _____

Overall my day was...

☺ ☺ ☹

Part I: To be filled out in the morning   Date: ____ / ____ / ____

My **happiness-source goals** for today are…

Something **meaningful**	Something **pleasurable**
Something **challenging**	Something **unpleasurable**

I am **grateful** for…

➕ _____

➕ _____

➕ _____

Part II: To be filled out at night

Two **happy moments** I had today were…

➕ _____

➕ _____

_____

An **act of kindness** I did today was…

➕ _____

_____

One **accomplishment** I had today was…

➕ _____

A **conscious struggle** I have is…

➕ _____

_____

_____

My **Happiness Trophy** goes to:

➕ _____

Overall my day was…

☺ 😐 ☹

Part I: To be filled out in the morning   Date: ____ / ____ / ____

My **happiness-source goals** for today are…

Something **meaningful**	Something **pleasurable**
Something **challenging**	Something **unpleasurable**

I am **grateful** for…

+ _____

+ _____

+ _____

Part II: To be filled out at night

Two **happy moments** I had today were…

+ _____

+ _____
_____

An **act of kindness** I did today was…

+ _____
_____

One **accomplishment** I had today was…

+ _____

A **conscious struggle** I have is…

+ _____
_____
_____

My **Happiness Trophy** goes to:

+ _____

Overall my day was…

☺ 😐 ☹

Part I: To be filled out in the morning   Date: ____ / ____ / ____

My **happiness-source goals** for today are...

Something **meaningful**	Something **pleasurable**
Something **challenging**	Something **unpleasurable**

I am **grateful** for...

+ _____

+ _____

+ _____

Part II: To be filled out at night

Two **happy moments** I had today were...

+ _____

+ _____

_____

An **act of kindness** I did today was...

+ _____

_____

A **conscious struggle** I have is...

+ _____

_____

_____

One **accomplishment** I had today was...

+ _____

My **Happiness Trophy** goes to:

+ _____

Overall my day was...

☺ ☺ ☹

Part I: To be filled out in the morning   Date: ____ / ____ / ____

My **happiness-source goals** for today are...

Something **meaningful**	Something **pleasurable**
Something **challenging**	Something **unpleasurable**

I am **grateful** for...

+ _____

+ _____

+ _____

Part II: To be filled out at night

Two **happy moments** I had today were...

+ _____

+ _____
_____

One **accomplishment** I had today was...

+ _____

My **Happiness Trophy** goes to:

+ _____

An **act of kindness** I did today was...

+ _____
_____

A **conscious struggle** I have is...

+ _____
_____
_____

Overall my day was...

☺ ☺ ☹

Part I: To be filled out in the morning   Date: _____ / _____ / _____

My **happiness-source goals** for today are...

Something **meaningful**	Something **pleasurable**
Something **challenging**	Something **unpleasurable**

I am **grateful** for...

+ _____

+ _____

+ _____

Part II: To be filled out at night

Two **happy moments** I had today were...

+ _____

+ _____

_____

An **act of kindness** I did today was...

+ _____

_____

One **accomplishment** I had today was...

+ _____

A **conscious struggle** I have is...

+ _____

_____

_____

My **Happiness Trophy** goes to:

+ _____

Overall my day was...

☺ ☺ ☹

Part I: To be filled out in the morning   Date: ____ / ____ / ____

My **happiness-source goals** for today are…

Something **meaningful**	Something **pleasurable**
Something **challenging**	Something **unpleasurable**

I am **grateful** for…

✦ _____

✦ _____

✦ _____

Part II: To be filled out at night

Two **happy moments** I had today were…

✦ _____

✦ _____

_____

An **act of kindness** I did today was…

✦ _____

_____

One **accomplishment** I had today was…

✦ _____

A **conscious struggle** I have is…

✦ _____

_____

_____

My **Happiness Trophy** goes to:

✦ _____

Overall my day was…

☺ 😐 ☹

Part I: To be filled out in the morning   Date: ____ / ____ / ____

My **happiness-source goals** for today are…

Something **meaningful**	Something **pleasurable**
Something **challenging**	Something **unpleasurable**

I am **grateful** for…

🔸 _____

🔸 _____

🔸 _____

Part II: To be filled out at night

Two **happy moments** I had today were…

🔸 _____

🔸 _____

_____

An **act of kindness** I did today was…

🔸 _____

_____

One **accomplishment** I had today was…

🔸 _____

A **conscious struggle** I have is…

🔸 _____

_____

_____

My **Happiness Trophy** goes to:

🔸 _____

Overall my day was…

☺ 😐 ☹

Part I: To be filled out in the morning   Date: ____ / ____ / ____

My **happiness-source goals** for today are…

Something **meaningful**	Something **pleasurable**
Something **challenging**	Something **unpleasurable**

I am **grateful** for…

+ _____

+ _____

+ _____

Part II: To be filled out at night

Two **happy moments** I had today were…

+ _____

+ _____

_____

An **act of kindness** I did today was…

+ _____

_____

One **accomplishment** I had today was…

+ _____

A **conscious struggle** I have is…

+ _____

_____

_____

My **Happiness Trophy** goes to:

+ _____

Overall my day was…

☺ ☺ ☹

Part I: To be filled out in the morning   Date: ____ / ____ / ____

My **happiness-source goals** for today are…

Something **meaningful**	Something **pleasurable**
Something **challenging**	Something **unpleasurable**

I am **grateful** for…

+ _____

+ _____

+ _____

Part II: To be filled out at night

Two **happy moments** I had today were…

+ _____

+ _____

An **act of kindness** I did today was…

+ _____

A **conscious struggle** I have is…

+ _____

One **accomplishment** I had today was…

+ _____

My **Happiness Trophy** goes to:

+ _____

Overall my day was…

☺ ☺ ☹

Part I: To be filled out in the morning   Date: _____ / _____ / _____

My **happiness-source goals** for today are…

Something **meaningful**	Something **pleasurable**
Something **challenging**	Something **unpleasurable**

I am **grateful** for…

* _____
* _____
* _____

Part II: To be filled out at night

Two **happy moments** I had today were…

* _____
* _____

One **accomplishment** I had today was…

* _____

My **Happiness Trophy** goes to:

* _____

An **act of kindness** I did today was…

* _____

A **conscious struggle** I have is…

* _____

Overall my day was…

☺ ☺ ☹

Part I: To be filled out in the morning   Date: ___ / ___ / ___

My **happiness-source goals** for today are...

Something **meaningful**	Something **pleasurable**
Something **challenging**	Something **unpleasurable**

I am **grateful** for...

+ _____

+ _____

+ _____

Part II: To be filled out at night

Two **happy moments** I had today were...

+ _____

+ _____

An **act of kindness** I did today was...

+ _____

One **accomplishment** I had today was...

+ _____

A **conscious struggle** I have is...

+ _____

My **Happiness Trophy** goes to:

+ _____

Overall my day was...

☺ ☺ ☹

Part I: To be filled out in the morning   Date: ____ / ____ / ____

My **happiness-source goals** for today are…

Something **meaningful**	Something **pleasurable**
Something **challenging**	Something **unpleasurable**

I am **grateful** for…

+ _____

+ _____

+ _____

Part II: To be filled out at night

Two **happy moments** I had today were…

+ _____

  _____

+ _____

  _____

An **act of kindness** I did today was…

+ _____

  _____

A **conscious struggle** I have is…

+ _____

  _____

  _____

One **accomplishment** I had today was…

+ _____

My **Happiness Trophy** goes to:

+ _____

Overall my day was…

☺ 😐 ☹

Part I: To be filled out in the morning   Date: ____ / ____ / ____

My **happiness-source goals** for today are…

Something **meaningful**	Something **pleasurable**
Something **challenging**	Something **unpleasurable**

I am **grateful** for…

+ _____

+ _____

+ _____

Part II: To be filled out at night

Two **happy moments** I had today were…

+ _____

+ _____

An **act of kindness** I did today was…

+ _____

One **accomplishment** I had today was…

+ _____

A **conscious struggle** I have is…

+ _____

My **Happiness Trophy** goes to:

+ _____

Overall my day was…

☺ ☺ ☹

Part I: To be filled out in the morning   Date: ____ / ____ / ____

My **happiness-source goals** for today are...

Something **meaningful**	Something **pleasurable**
Something **challenging**	Something **unpleasurable**

I am **grateful** for...

+ _____

+ _____

+ _____

Part II: To be filled out at night

Two **happy moments** I had today were...

+ _____

+ _____

An **act of kindness** I did today was...

+ _____

One **accomplishment** I had today was...

+ _____

A **conscious struggle** I have is...

+ _____

My **Happiness Trophy** goes to:

+ _____

Overall my day was...

☺ ☺ ☹

Part I: To be filled out in the morning   Date: _____ / _____ / _____

My **happiness-source goals** for today are...

Something **meaningful**	Something **pleasurable**
Something **challenging**	Something **unpleasurable**

I am **grateful** for...

🌿 _____

🌿 _____

🌿 _____

Part II: To be filled out at night

Two **happy moments** I had today were...

🌿 _____

🌿 _____

_____

An **act of kindness** I did today was...

🌿 _____

_____

One **accomplishment** I had today was...

🌿 _____

A **conscious struggle** I have is...

🌿 _____

_____

_____

My **Happiness Trophy** goes to:

🌿 _____

Overall my day was...

☺ 😐 ☹

Part I: To be filled out in the morning   Date: _____ / _____ / _____

My **happiness-source goals** for today are…

Something **meaningful**	Something **pleasurable**
Something **challenging**	Something **unpleasurable**

I am **grateful** for…

🔸 _____

🔸 _____

🔸 _____

Part II: To be filled out at night

Two **happy moments** I had today were…

🔸 _____

🔸 _____

_____

An **act of kindness** I did today was…

🔸 _____

_____

A **conscious struggle** I have is…

🔸 _____

_____

_____

One **accomplishment** I had today was…

🔸 _____

My **Happiness Trophy** goes to:

🔸 _____

Overall my day was…

☺ ☺ ☹

Part I: To be filled out in the morning   Date: _____ / _____ / _____

My **happiness-source goals** for today are…

Something **meaningful**	Something **pleasurable**
Something **challenging**	Something **unpleasurable**

I am **grateful** for…

+ _____
+ _____
+ _____

Part II: To be filled out at night

Two **happy moments** I had today were…

+ _____
+ _____
  _____

An **act of kindness** I did today was…

+ _____
  _____

One **accomplishment** I had today was…

+ _____

A **conscious struggle** I have is…

+ _____
  _____
  _____

My **Happiness Trophy** goes to:

+ _____

Overall my day was…

☺ 😐 ☹

Part I: To be filled out in the morning   Date: ____ / ____ / ____

My **happiness-source goals** for today are…

Something **meaningful**	Something **pleasurable**
Something **challenging**	Something **unpleasurable**

I am **grateful** for…

+ _____
+ _____
+ _____

Part II: To be filled out at night

Two **happy moments** I had today were…
+ _____
+ _____

An **act of kindness** I did today was…
+ _____
_____

One **accomplishment** I had today was…
+ _____

A **conscious struggle** I have is…
+ _____
_____
_____

My **Happiness Trophy** goes to:
+ _____

Overall my day was…

☺ 😐 ☹

Part I: To be filled out in the morning   Date: ____ / ____ / ____

My **happiness-source goals** for today are…

Something **meaningful**	Something **pleasurable**
Something **challenging**	Something **unpleasurable**

I am **grateful** for…

_____

_____

_____

Part II: To be filled out at night

Two **happy moments** I had today were…

_____

_____

_____

One **accomplishment** I had today was…

_____

My **Happiness Trophy** goes to:

_____

An **act of kindness** I did today was…

_____

_____

A **conscious struggle** I have is…

_____

_____

_____

Overall my day was…

☺ 😐 ☹

Part I: To be filled out in the morning   Date: ____ / ____ / ____

My **happiness-source goals** for today are...

Something **meaningful**	Something **pleasurable**
Something **challenging**	Something **unpleasurable**

I am **grateful** for...

✦ _____

✦ _____

✦ _____

Part II: To be filled out at night

Two **happy moments** I had today were...

✦ _____

✦ _____

_____

An **act of kindness** I did today was...

✦ _____

_____

One **accomplishment** I had today was...

✦ _____

A **conscious struggle** I have is...

✦ _____

_____

_____

My **Happiness Trophy** goes to:

✦ _____

Overall my day was...

☺ 😐 ☹

Part I: To be filled out in the morning   Date: ____ / ____ / ____

My **happiness-source goals** for today are...

Something **meaningful**	Something **pleasurable**
Something **challenging**	Something **unpleasurable**

I am **grateful** for...

- _____
- _____
- _____

Part II: To be filled out at night

Two **happy moments** I had today were...
- _____
- _____
  _____

An **act of kindness** I did today was...
- _____
  _____

One **accomplishment** I had today was...
- _____

A **conscious struggle** I have is...
- _____
  _____

My **Happiness Trophy** goes to:
- _____

Overall my day was...

☺ ☻ ☹

Part I: To be filled out in the morning   Date: ____ / ____ / ____

My **happiness-source goals** for today are...

Something **meaningful**	Something **pleasurable**
Something **challenging**	Something **unpleasurable**

I am **grateful** for...

+ _____
+ _____
+ _____

Part II: To be filled out at night

Two **happy moments** I had today were...

+ _____
+ _____
  _____

An **act of kindness** I did today was...

+ _____
  _____

One **accomplishment** I had today was...

+ _____

A **conscious struggle** I have is...

+ _____
  _____
  _____

My **Happiness Trophy** goes to:

+ _____

Overall my day was...

☺ ☺ ☹

Part I: To be filled out in the morning   Date: ____ / ____ / ____

My **happiness-source goals** for today are...

Something **meaningful**	Something **pleasurable**
Something **challenging**	Something **unpleasurable**

I am **grateful** for...

- _____
- _____
- _____

Part II: To be filled out at night

Two **happy moments** I had today were...
- _____
- _____

An **act of kindness** I did today was...
- _____
  _____

One **accomplishment** I had today was...
- _____

A **conscious struggle** I have is...
- _____
  _____

My **Happiness Trophy** goes to:
- _____

Overall my day was...

☺ ☺ ☹

Part I: To be filled out in the morning   Date: ____ / ____ / ____

My **happiness-source goals** for today are...

Something **meaningful**	Something **pleasurable**
Something **challenging**	Something **unpleasurable**

I am **grateful** for...

+ _____

+ _____

+ _____

Part II: To be filled out at night

Two **happy moments** I had today were...

+ _____

+ _____

An **act of kindness** I did today was...

+ _____

_____

One **accomplishment** I had today was...

+ _____

A **conscious struggle** I have is...

+ _____

_____

_____

My **Happiness Trophy** goes to:

+ _____

Overall my day was...

☺ ☺ ☹

Part I: To be filled out in the morning   Date: _____ / _____ / _____

My **happiness-source goals** for today are…

Something **meaningful**	Something **pleasurable**
Something **challenging**	Something **unpleasurable**

I am **grateful** for…

+ _____

+ _____

+ _____

Part II: To be filled out at night

Two **happy moments** I had today were…

+ _____

+ _____

_____

An **act of kindness** I did today was…

+ _____

_____

One **accomplishment** I had today was…

+ _____

A **conscious struggle** I have is…

+ _____

_____

My **Happiness Trophy** goes to:

+ _____

Overall my day was...

☺ ☹ ☹

214

Part I: To be filled out in the morning   Date: ____ / ____ / ____

My **happiness-source goals** for today are...

Something **meaningful**	Something **pleasurable**
Something **challenging**	Something **unpleasurable**

I am **grateful** for...

✦ _____

✦ _____

✦ _____

Part II: To be filled out at night

Two **happy moments** I had today were...

✦ _____

✦ _____

_____

An **act of kindness** I did today was...

✦ _____

_____

One **accomplishment** I had today was...

✦ _____

A **conscious struggle** I have is...

✦ _____

_____

_____

My **Happiness Trophy** goes to:

✦ _____

Overall my day was...

☺ 😐 ☹

Part I: To be filled out in the morning   Date: _____ / _____ / _____

My **happiness-source goals** for today are...

Something **meaningful**	Something **pleasurable**
Something **challenging**	Something **unpleasurable**

I am **grateful** for...

+ _____

+ _____

+ _____

Part II: To be filled out at night

Two **happy moments** I had today were...

+ _____

+ _____

_____

One **accomplishment** I had today was...

+ _____

My **Happiness Trophy** goes to:

+ _____

An **act of kindness** I did today was...

+ _____

_____

A **conscious struggle** I have is...

+ _____

_____

_____

Overall my day was...

☺ ☺ ☹

Part I: To be filled out in the morning   Date: _____ / _____ / _____

My **happiness-source goals** for today are…

Something **meaningful**	Something **pleasurable**
Something **challenging**	Something **unpleasurable**

I am **grateful** for…

+ _____

+ _____

+ _____

Part II: To be filled out at night

Two **happy moments** I had today were…

+ _____
+ _____
_____

An **act of kindness** I did today was…

+ _____
_____

One **accomplishment** I had today was…

+ _____

A **conscious struggle** I have is…

+ _____
_____
_____

My **Happiness Trophy** goes to:

+ _____

Overall my day was…

☺ ☺ ☹

Part I: To be filled out in the morning   Date: _____ / _____ / _____

My **happiness-source goals** for today are…

Something **meaningful**	Something **pleasurable**
Something **challenging**	Something **unpleasurable**

I am **grateful** for…

⚓ _____

⚓ _____

⚓ _____

Part II: To be filled out at night

Two **happy moments** I had today were…

⚓ _____

⚓ _____
_____

An **act of kindness** I did today was…

⚓ _____
_____

One **accomplishment** I had today was…

⚓ _____

A **conscious struggle** I have is…

⚓ _____
_____
_____

My **Happiness Trophy** goes to:

⚓ _____

Overall my day was…

☺ ☺ ☹

Part I: To be filled out in the morning   Date: ____ / ____ / ____

My **happiness-source goals** for today are...

Something **meaningful**	Something **pleasurable**
Something **challenging**	Something **unpleasurable**

I am **grateful** for...

- _____
- _____
- _____

Part II: To be filled out at night

Two **happy moments** I had today were...

- _____
- _____
_____

An **act of kindness** I did today was...

- _____
_____

One **accomplishment** I had today was...

- _____

A **conscious struggle** I have is...

- _____
_____
_____

My **Happiness Trophy** goes to:

- _____

Overall my day was...

☺ ☺ ☹

Part I: To be filled out in the morning   Date: _____ / _____ / _____

My **happiness-source goals** for today are…

Something **meaningful**	Something **pleasurable**
Something **challenging**	Something **unpleasurable**

I am **grateful** for…

🕇 _____

🕇 _____

🕇 _____

Part II: To be filled out at night

Two **happy moments** I had today were…

🕇 _____

🕇 _____

_____

An **act of kindness** I did today was…

🕇 _____

_____

One **accomplishment** I had today was…

🕇 _____

A **conscious struggle** I have is…

🕇 _____

_____

_____

My **Happiness Trophy** goes to:

🕇 _____

Overall my day was…

☺ 😐 ☹

Part I: To be filled out in the morning   Date: ____ / ____ / ____

My **happiness-source goals** for today are...

Something **meaningful**	Something **pleasurable**
Something **challenging**	Something **unpleasurable**

I am **grateful** for...

+ _____

+ _____

+ _____

Part II: To be filled out at night

Two **happy moments** I had today were...

+ _____

+ _____

An **act of kindness** I did today was...

+ _____

_____

One **accomplishment** I had today was...

+ _____

A **conscious struggle** I have is...

+ _____

_____

_____

My **Happiness Trophy** goes to:

+ _____

Overall my day was...

☺ ☺ ☹

Part I: To be filled out in the morning   Date: _____ / _____ / _____

My **happiness-source goals** for today are...

Something **meaningful**	Something **pleasurable**
Something **challenging**	Something **unpleasurable**

I am **grateful** for...

+ _____

+ _____

+ _____

Part II: To be filled out at night

Two **happy moments** I had today were...

+ _____

+ _____

_____

An **act of kindness** I did today was...

+ _____

_____

One **accomplishment** I had today was...

+ _____

A **conscious struggle** I have is...

+ _____

_____

_____

My **Happiness Trophy** goes to:

+ _____

Overall my day was...

☺ ☹ ☹

Part I: To be filled out in the morning   Date: ____ / ____ / ____

My **happiness-source goals** for today are…

Something **meaningful**	Something **pleasurable**
Something **challenging**	Something **unpleasurable**

I am **grateful** for…

+ _____

+ _____

+ _____

Part II: To be filled out at night

Two **happy moments** I had today were…

+ _____

+ _____
_____

An **act of kindness** I did today was…

+ _____
_____

One **accomplishment** I had today was…

+ _____

A **conscious struggle** I have is…

+ _____
_____
_____

My **Happiness Trophy** goes to:

+ _____

Overall my day was…

☺ ☺ ☹

Part I: To be filled out in the morning   Date: ____ / ____ / ____

My **happiness-source goals** for today are…

Something **meaningful**	Something **pleasurable**
Something **challenging**	Something **unpleasurable**

I am **grateful** for…

- _____
- _____
- _____

Part II: To be filled out at night

Two **happy moments** I had today were…
- _____
- _____

An **act of kindness** I did today was…
- _____

One **accomplishment** I had today was…
- _____

A **conscious struggle** I have is…
- _____

My **Happiness Trophy** goes to:
- _____

Overall my day was…

☺ 😐 ☹

Part I: To be filled out in the morning   Date: _____ / _____ / _____

My **happiness-source goals** for today are…

Something **meaningful**	Something **pleasurable**
Something **challenging**	Something **unpleasurable**

I am **grateful** for…

✦ _____

✦ _____

✦ _____

Part II: To be filled out at night

Two **happy moments** I had today were…

✦ _____

✦ _____

_____

An **act of kindness** I did today was…

✦ _____

_____

One **accomplishment** I had today was…

✦ _____

A **conscious struggle** I have is…

✦ _____

_____

_____

My **Happiness Trophy** goes to:

✦ _____

Overall my day was…

☺ ☺ ☹

Part I: To be filled out in the morning   Date: ____ / ____ / ____

My **happiness-source goals** for today are...

Something **meaningful**	Something **pleasurable**
Something **challenging**	Something **unpleasurable**

I am **grateful** for...

_____

_____

_____

Part II: To be filled out at night

Two **happy moments** I had today were...

_____

_____

An **act of kindness** I did today was...

_____

_____

One **accomplishment** I had today was...

_____

A **conscious struggle** I have is...

_____

_____

_____

My **Happiness Trophy** goes to:

_____

Overall my day was...

☺ ☺ ☹

Part I: To be filled out in the morning   Date: ____ / ____ / ____

My **happiness-source goals** for today are...

Something **meaningful**	Something **pleasurable**
Something **challenging**	Something **unpleasurable**

I am **grateful** for...

➤ _____

➤ _____

➤ _____

Part II: To be filled out at night

Two **happy moments** I had today were...

➤ _____

_____

➤ _____

_____

An **act of kindness** I did today was...

➤ _____

_____

A **conscious struggle** I have is...

➤ _____

_____

_____

One **accomplishment** I had today was...

➤ _____

My **Happiness Trophy** goes to:

➤ _____

Overall my day was...

☺ ☺ ☹

Refill your way to a purposeful and mindful life now that you found sustained happiness. Continue your journey by reordering My Happiness Habit Journal
(also available on Amazon).

About The Author

Angelica Ribeiro is the author of *Running into Happiness: How My Happiness Habit Journal Created Lasting Happiness in the Midst of a Crazy-busy Semester*. She holds a master's degree in multicultural education from the University of Massachusetts Amherst. She has worked with English learners and preservice teachers in the United States and Brazil for over seventeen years.

Currently a PhD candidate at Texas A&M University, Ribeiro studies curriculum and instruction with a focus on English as a second language. She also works as a professor in higher-education and helps others benefit from her happiness research. She lives in Houston, Texas.

54713664R00128

Made in the USA
Columbia, SC
04 April 2019